"We live in a new, technolog [barcode] young women navigate the mi. M000033121 every direction. With conversational style and much-needed humor, Hall invites young women and teens to discover and understand that their worth and fulfillment in life does not come from how many followers one may have, or some perfect romance. With a continuous message emphasized through-out: *You matter. Your life matters.* And your influence matters, no matter your age. Through personal stories and anecdotes, Hall takes readers on an inward journey to discover their own unique talents and gifts, and she invites readers to embrace their faith in a new way. I was literally laughing out loud at parts and nodding my head in agreement throughout. Simply so needed in today's social media-driven world, this book helps readers understand what is 'real,' what really matters in the big picture, and how to become a true, life-long 'influencer.' I wish I had this book when I was a teen."

–Kim Childress, book editor at *Girls' Life Magazine*

"In a world where identity and purpose are challenged in every area for teens, *Influencer* is the answer for them to discover how to impact our world for God's glory. Tessa unpacks the exact steps a teen can journey through to find the gifts God gave them, fulfill their call only they can fill, and walk into their destiny with significant influence. *Influencer* is a must-read for every teen!"

–Laine Lawson Craft, best-selling and award-winning author, *Warfare Parenting* podcast host, popular media host, and speaker

"Tessa Hall speaks to the longing in every teen's heart, reminding them they have value, purpose, and influence because the King of the Universe calls them His daughters, royal, chosen, and holy. Culture will tell us all the ways we are lacking, but Hall reminds us that we are more than enough, because Jesus says we're wonderful. Jesus set each of us apart to do good work for Him and empowered those who love Him to do incredible things. And knowing this, we can influence the world with His love and light."

—Laura L. Smith, speaker and best-selling author
of *Restore My Soul* and *5 Minute Devotions for
Teens: A Guide to God and Mental Health*

"Almost all of us have wondered what our calling is and how to honor God with our lives. We wonder if we should be traveling overseas to feed hungry children, or sharing the gospel with hundreds of people from stages. Tessa encourages teen girls (and this thirty-something stay-at-home mom) that we can live God's unique and beautiful calling right now. We don't need to do what everyone else is doing to make a difference. We can use the gifts God has given us to shine a light in this dark world starting today. This book is for the dreamer with a God-shaped heart."

—Shelbie Mae, author of *Girls Like Me: 12
Short Bible Studies About Biblical Women*

"Relevant, relatable, and full of heart, *Influencer* challenges teens to embrace their God-given identities. In a media-centric world, it's easy to lose sight of one's true purpose and value. Tessa Emily Hall guides readers on a journey to see themselves from God's perspective and claim the unique callings placed on their lives. A fresh addition to any bookshelf. Tessa is a breakout voice."

–Caroline Georgia, multi-published author of
YA fiction including *Dearest Josephine*

"Influencer takes you on a journey to discover the potential that we all carry within us to impact this world. Maybe you do not feel like you are making a big impact? In a culture that can easily drag us down with volumes of perfectionism and false personas, Tessa gets to the depth of who we are and our great need for security in Christ. Tessa is humorous, authentic, and motivating. This is a must-read for every young woman to help grow in their confidence and joy in the unique path that the Lord has for their lives. This book creates the space for you to process and pray through your own purpose. *Influencer* encourages us that there is no age requirement in the kingdom of God, our time is now."

–Emma Danzey, author of *Wildflower: Blooming Through Singleness* & podcast host of Her Many Hats

"Influencer is a delightful and easy-to-read encouragement to the struggles and triumphs of a life with Christ in today's world. Tessa has a charming way of writing that speaks directly to the heart, while also capturing the interest with relatable anecdotes and girl talk that cuts right through the chaos of the teen years and speaks life and truth to this generation."

–Victoria Lynn, multi-published author of Christian
fantasy including The Chronicles of Elira Series

"Tessa Emily Hall brings a fun, fresh, and much-needed voice of truth to today's teens! The highly relatable and heartfelt stories that Tessa shares in this book will make readers feel like they're sitting down for a cozy cup of coffee and an encouraging, heart-to-heart chat with an old friend! In a world that's tempting teens to drift further and further from the truth of God's Word, *Influencer* will serve as an anchor to reinforce biblical realities and kingdom culture in the hearts and minds of all who read it!"

–Olivia Lynn Jarmusch, YA Christian fiction author
of *The Tales of Tarsurella* and *Regal Hearts*

"Who DOESN'T want to be an influencer? In this book, Tessa Emily Hall uses a non-preachy, conversational tone to help you realize your potential to impact the world for eternity. A must-read for any teen!"

–Bekah Hamrick Martin, author of *The Bare Naked Truth, NIV Adventure Bible Book of Devotions,* and *The Teen NIV Bible Study Notes*

Influencer

A Teen Girl's Invitation to a Life of Purpose-Driven Impact

Tessa Emily Hall

END GAME
Press

End Game Press books may be purchased in bulk at special discounts for sales promotion, corpo-
rate gifts, ministry, fund-raising, or educational purposes. Special editions can also be created to
specifications. For details, contact Special Sales Dept., End Game Press, P.O. Box 206, Nesbit, MS
38651 or info@endgamepress.com.

Visit our website at www.endgamepress.com.

Library of Congress Control Number: 2022952476
Hardback ISBN: 978-1-63797-102-4
Paperback ISBN: 978-1-63797-103-1
eBook ISBN: 978-1-63797-101-7

Cover Design by Hannah Mae Linder
Interior Design by Typewriter Creative Co.

Published in association with Cyle Young of the Cyle Young Literary Elite, LLC.

Scriptures marked NIV are taken from The New International Version (NIV): Scripture Taken
From The Holy Bible, New International Version ®. Copyright© 1973, 1978, 1984, 2011 By
Biblica, Inc.™. Used by permission of Zondervan. All rights reserved worldwide. www.zondervan.
com The "NIV" and "New International Version" are trademarks registered in the United States
Patent and Trademark Office by Biblica, Inc.™

"Scripture quotations marked (ESV) are from The ESV® Bible (The Holy Bible, English Standard
Version®), copyright © 2001 by Crossway, a publishing ministry of Good News Publishers. Used
by permission. All rights reserved."

Scripture quotations are taken from the Holy Bible, New Living Translation, copyright ©1996,
2004, 2015 by Tyndale House Foundation. Used by permission of Tyndale House Publishers,
Carol Stream, Illinois 60188. All rights reserved.

Scripture quotations marked MSG are taken from THE MESSAGE, copyright © 1993, 2002,
2018 by Eugene H. Peterson. Used by permission of NavPress, represented by Tyndale House
Publishers. All rights reserved.

Scripture quotations marked TPT are from The Passion Translation®. Copyright © 2017,
2018, 2020 by Passion & Fire Ministries, Inc. Used by permission. All rights reserved.
ThePassionTranslation.com.

Taken from the Holy Bible: Easy-to-Read Version (ERV), International Edition © 2013, 2016 by
Bible League International and used by permission.

Printed in India
10 9 8 7 6 5 4 3 2 1

To Nusa Rae Brose, my one and only niece—a courageous little toddler who never backs down from an adventure. You are a leader in the making, Nusa, just like I have prayed. Your greatest adventure will be embarked as you carry out God's calling on your life, and I can't wait to witness the impact your little hands will someday make on this world.

Your Aunt Tessa loves you very much! <3

Table of Contents

Introduction

Dear [insert your name here],

You have been invited to serve as influencer.

No, I'm not referring to the *social media* kind of influencer. You know, those TikTokers who make a living from being an online ambassador for brands and businesses—beautiful people who create a simple post and can influence their thousands of followers to purchase a product. This role you've been offered is far superior. Because the influence you can make isn't going to just impact your social media following.

It can impact the *world*.

This role as an influencer will infuse your life with meaning and help you to live out your divine destiny. Beginning while you're still a teenager. And the best part is? You don't even need a social media presence if that's not your thing. Yes, you heard me correctly. There's no need to spend your days snapping photos and trying to persuade your followers to buy a product. (Unless you want to, of course.)

You see, this position as an influencer isn't even one you

need to strive hard to earn. Your acceptance isn't based on popularity, appearance, or even intelligence. This position was *designed* for you. Quite literally, actually! Every aspect that makes you *you* was chosen with intention so you could carry out your unique assignment. (You'll learn more about assignments in part two.)

So, really, there's no need to even apply for this role, because this invitation was presented to you thousands of years ago.

And it's in this role as influencer that you will discover your reason for being on this earth. This God-given calling of yours will give you a sense of excitement and purpose for your future—and your *present*. You'll learn how to discover your gifts and use them to the fullest potential, even if you're convinced you don't have any. (Spoiler alert: *You do.)*

Are you ready to have a sneak peek at what God could have in store for you? Do you want to learn how to make the most of your teen years while taking advantage of the influence you already have as a young person?

If so, it's time to accept your role as influencer.

Let's begin!

Part One
Accepting the Invitation

Chapter One
Fairy Tale Romance

*C*an I share a secret with you?

I'll go ahead and cut to the chase:

I haven't dated a guy in almost ten years—and I'm in my late twenties. Sounds crazy, right?

Now, don't worry. This isn't a book about dating or relationships. And I'm not sharing so you'll feel sorry for me, because really, I'm doing perfectly fine without a man for the time being, *thankyouverymuch*. The only reason I even started this book by exposing my secret is so you'll believe me when I say this:

That void inside of me—the yearning I once had for earthly romance—is no longer a crater inside of my heart, sucking away my life. I once thought if I wasn't married by my mid-twenties, then I'd be unfulfilled. Like I'd have that something-is-missing kind of feeling that would cast dark shadows onto my everyday life. You know how when it's cloudy outside, the lack of sun may cause you to go throughout the entire day in a gloomy and lethargic kind of mood? It's like the sun has the power to brighten our day…literally and figuratively. And its *lack* of presence, on the other hand, drains the life out of it.

I assumed the absence of a husband in my life would be like that, in a sense. Like I'd live a dull and empty life until Mr. Future Husband finally made his grand arrival.

But now I laugh at myself for giving earthly romance far more credit than it deserves. I blame it on the steady diet of happily-ever-after Disney princess movies I consumed growing up. At the beginning of those films, the princess (or soon-to-be princess) often lived an average life…until she met her prince. And then it's as though that new romance became the key to helping her blossom from an average girl into a beautiful and poised young woman.

Truth is, that's not typically how romance works on the other side of the movie screen. Back here in the reality universe, it's not a prince that causes young women to discover their full potential. A prince doesn't have the power to transition a young lady's life from gloom and doom to bright and sunny.

Now, before I have the chance to burst your bubble entirely—if I haven't already—I will share with you one thing those movies did right:

Love does, in fact, bring out the best in us. Love defines who we are.

Yet it's only the eternal kind of love has this power.

It's an eternal kind of love that can wave a magic wand over our lives and transform us from average into royalty;

from living in the dark shadows of hopelessness to basking in an eternal light.

Curious to find out how you can receive this kind of love? Read on.

Ecstasy of Love

Before we continue further in the book, let's do a quick imagination exercise. Is that fine with you? Great. Take a moment and close your eyes. Wait—on second thought, that might make reading quite a challenge, so keep them open please.

Imagine you're Eve, the first woman to ever step foot on this earth. Life is radiant, and the Garden of Eden has not yet been tampered with by time. The blades of grass tickle your bare feet, their warmth a byproduct of the powerful presence of God even more than of the endless sunlight. The ripe fruit growing along the trees and the breathtaking beauty of flowers blooming along shrubbery splashes the earth with vibrant hues of the rainbow. The sweet aroma entices you. A stream trickles with life-giving water nearby, and the cool breeze whisks your long hair behind your back.

The threat of being attacked by a wild animal has never once entered your mind, and you have never tasted bitterness—literally nor figuratively. Endless energy zaps through your body, the kind of invigoration that can only be provided by perfect health. It's this vigor that provides you the ability to work and enjoy communion with your husband, Adam, as well as your Creator, God.

You were not raised by earthly parents, yet somehow you have always known it was God who created you. You were born with the awareness that it is *because* of God you were created, it is *through* Him you continue to be sustained, and it is *for* Him you were placed on this earth. His endless perfection and presence showers the garden in a constant ray of eternal light and love. There is nothing you could do that would add more beauty to the Garden.

You breathe in the fresh, earthy air and release a slow exhale, God's love seeping through your veins. *Love* is all you have ever known. It flows in you, through you, and all around you—coming from the very core of your being, where He abides.

The sun reaches its rays above the distant horizon, and you shield your eyes as you take in the Garden and give thanks to God. Birds flap their wings above you, joining with the rest of creation in singing praise to the Creator. Joy bubbles up inside your chest, and you can't help but burst into a smile, overwhelmed by this eternal ecstasy of love.

Sounds like quite an ideal life, wouldn't you agree?

You may already be aware this is only the prologue to life as we know it today. Our world didn't remain at this level of perfection.

To make a long story short—as many believers know— the Enemy, who disguised himself in the body of a serpent, slithered by and cunningly deceived Eve, tricking her into sinning against God; thus, the perfect world Adam and Eve once knew became forever tainted with the stench of death and suffering. Mankind became cursed from this fall, and destruction fell upon the land. (You can read the entire story in Genesis 1–3.)

Don't you know Eve's heart longed—ached, even—to return to the perfection of the Garden of Eden she once enjoyed?

Unfortunately, God forbid she and her husband ever step foot into the Garden again. But I doubt it was even the ecstasy of the Garden Eve missed the most.

It was the ecstasy of love.

The kind that could only be provided through deep fellowship with her Creator.

Making Up for the Loss

Perhaps you already know how the rest of this story plays out—how God sent His Son, Jesus, to earth so humankind could once again live in deep fellowship with the Creator. Jesus chose to receive the curse separating us from God in place of mankind when He hung on the cross, pouring Himself out as a sacrifice so we could receive this gift of eternal life.

Have you ever wondered why God went through all this trouble? I mean, He could have simply left humankind wandering around in the curse of sin and suffering throughout all eternity. He could have said something like, "It's not my problem! You're the ones who got yourselves into this mess. Good luck surviving in this miserable, hopeless world."

But that was never His attitude. God's heart ached, longing to have intimacy with His creation without the barriers of sin. And He knew there was no other way than through Jesus. There was no Plan B when it came to restoring mankind back to the Creator. For us to enjoy eternal life with God, He would need to send His Son, Jesus—God in flesh—to receive the weight of evil, sin, and suffering in our place. All of which was introduced to this world because of the serpent.

That was a demonstration of just how much God cherishes personal relationship with His children. We are reminded of this in 1 John 4:9:

"God showed how much he loved us by sending his one and only Son into the world so that we might have eternal life through him."

I believe it pains God for Him to witness us roaming around on our own. Void of life, love, and hope—the gifts Jesus came to restore to us. But I also don't judge anyone for searching the world in an attempt to satisfy their deepest longings, either. After all, there is a God-shaped hole inside each of us, and it's not until we have a relationship with Jesus that we will receive the only kind of love powerful enough to fill that emptiness.

The journey of discovering our life's purpose is going to be fruitless unless it *begins and ends with our relationship with Christ.* It is only by establishing this relationship that we find the purpose for which we were created.

And that involves nothing less than walking in communion with God.

The same ecstasy of love Eve experienced in the Garden of Eden.

Your Invitation

What if I approached you and said, "Hey [insert your name here], I know of a guy who would be perfect for you. Not only that, but he is actually in love with you already and has even decided you are his bride. Your wedding is scheduled for this Saturday. Good luck! Oh, and don't forget your wedding dress!"

You'd probably be like, "Um, thanks, but I'd kind of like to have a chance to fall in love with the person I choose to marry. Scratch that: I'd like to at least get to know him first! Are you nuts?"

Fortunately, women here in the States generally have the freedom to choose to marry men whom they are in love with (as opposed to some cultures that arrange marriages). Love should be the driving factor behind a romantic relationship.

In the same way, love should be the driving factor behind our devotion to God as well. He would never force us to love Him. How could that possibly be love? Instead, He has given us free will. We can *choose* to cultivate a relationship with Him and accept His invitation of love.

Or we can walk away from His offer and miss out on the same ecstasy of love Adam and Eve cherished in the Garden of Eden. We can live life on our own and miss out on the divine plan He has in store for our lives.

It's our choice.

I, for one, hope you do decide to accept this invitation. This begins by understanding the price Jesus paid for you on Calvary (which you can read about in Matthew 27:1–54 and Mark 15:1–40) and then taking intentional effort to cultivate an ongoing relationship with Him.

If you're ready to accept Jesus into your heart for the first time, I'd advise you to turn to the section at the end of this book titled "Accepting Jesus as Your Personal Savior." Go ahead and do that now before continuing. Don't worry, it's not long, and I'll still be here waiting for your return.

Back now? Perfect. If you just accepted Jesus into your heart for the very first time, let me be the first to offer you a huge congratulations! Well, not actually the first, because Luke 15:10 says even the angels in heaven rejoice when a sinner comes into repentance. If we were talking in person, I'd embrace you with a hug and offer you chocolate. Or if you're one of those "unique" people who don't like chocolate, I'd reward you with your favorite coffee drink instead. And if you're not a fan of chocolate or coffee, then, well...I'd just rather not know.

You are now a "new creation" in Christ, according to 2 Corinthians 5:17. Christ lives within you. Nothing you do or walk through in life will ever be strong enough to cast you away from His presence. If you choose to live your life for Christ, trust me: You will be in for the adventure of a lifetime!

Now here's the fun part. You see, a lot of people simply say a prayer of salvation and then that's all. They miss out on cultivating an ongoing, day-to-day relationship with Jesus Christ.

I don't want you to be one of those people.

Instead, I want you to experience the same fairy tale romance I have. Remember me telling you about how God's eternal love has replaced that life-sucking void inside of me? How it's only through the power of His love I have discovered my identity, my purpose, my reason for being on this earth?

It's true. The same can happen for you as well.

And not even the best happily-ever-after storytellers could write a more romantic love story than the one you're about to experience.

Chapter Two
The Only Fuel We Need

I hate to admit it, but when I was a kid, I dreaded going to church on Sunday mornings. The idea of waking up early on the weekend and wearing a dress my mom chose for me (dresses were *not* my thing back then) was almost as unappetizing as eating carrots. And that's saying a lot considering how much I despised carrots. I didn't even appreciate the fun ways the children's pastor tried to make children's church exciting for kids—such as allowing us to play games like Red Light, Green Light. Passing out Goldfish® crackers for us to snack on while Veggie Tales played. Or holding performances for the 90s hit Christian song "Big House".

Growing up, going to church was just another weekly activity in my daily life—like attending school, brushing my hair, or taking a bath in the evening. As a kid, you don't make many decisions on your own, and this was one of those things for me. Maybe it was for you as well.

Fast forward several years. The fourteen-year-old me no longer dreaded church; instead, she looked forward to it.

What is it that marked this transition in my attitude, you ask?

Well, at first, I didn't have the drive nor the enthusiasm to go to church.

You know how, when you were a kid, it didn't take a lot of motivation to hop out of bed on Christmas mornings? Back then, the anticipation of seeing our presents drove us to get up and get moving.

Church was just another activity I did when my parents were in charge. But middle school ushered in a lonely season into my life, one that compelled me to reach out to God on my own. *Without* my parents' guidance this time. I was desperate for His love. Desperate for hope.

In this desperation, I found Jesus.

In Jesus, I found eternal love.

And in eternal love, I received the fuel—the motivation—to live for Him, which included going to church on Sunday mornings.

You see, it's love, not religion, that will empower us to live a life of meaning and impact.

So once you've accepted Christ as your Savior, how can you keep yourselves replenished so you don't miss out on God's perfect will for your life?

Love Makes the Difference

There's a famous actor who also experienced what it's like to journey through life in both conditions of the heart: empty and fueled. He's familiar with the adrenaline-pumping shift that consumes you when you finally receive the *right* kind of motivation.

Growing up, however, this actor didn't even go to church. He placed Jesus in the same category as Santa Claus and the Easter Bunny.[1] In his perspective, Christ was just another figment of people's imagination.

This actor's name is Kirk Cameron. Your parents may have seen him on the sitcom *Growing Pains* when he was a teenager.

It wasn't until Kirk was seventeen he accepted an invitation to have a relationship with Jesus—and all because he was trying to impress a girl he liked, a girl who had invited him to church. (Hey, I give him props for striving to go through God to get a girl!) Accepting the invitation to receive Christ as his Savior was the starting point for him. He discovered Christianity wasn't a make-believe religion; it was a relationship. And this relationship was far more meaningful than any earthly romance.[2]

This newfound love Kirk Cameron discovered in Jesus Christ fueled his heart to live for God. It cleansed his eyes, granting him new sight, enabling him to see with a transformed perspective. From this new sight, he could now see how everything in his life—including the early fame, success, and riches—had left him empty.

Sure, he may have thought all the attention was empowering him. But everyone knows cars can go only so far down the road without receiving the *proper* kind of gas.

Kirk Cameron once said in an interview, "I can honestly tell you today of all the places I've ever been, of all the people I've ever met, of all the fun and exciting things I've ever done, absolutely nothing compares to the joy of knowing Jesus Christ, of knowing my sins are forgiven and I'm in a right relationship with God."[3]

Isn't that crazy? I mean, here's an actor who seemed to have had it all according to the world's viewpoint. He didn't need to fret over his bank account. Girls adored him. His career was set in stone for the future. What else could he possibly need to live a happy life?

But after discovering the real fuel, he realized the fake stuff was only temporary. It couldn't sustain him long-term. It couldn't even compare. Because all the success in the world would never infuse his life with purpose, meaning, and peace the way Jesus did.

Love made the difference for Kirk Cameron. It granted him the "joy" he spoke about, and that joy unveiled an entirely new purpose for his life. That joy propelled him to continue living for God to this day as an influencer for Christ in Hollywood.

Did you know this was the same fuel that empowered Jesus to face the cross as well? Many of us will do everything we can to get out of doing something difficult. Maybe you've even faked a cold to avoid taking a difficult exam at school. And yet even the most painful, challenging, and uncomfortable moments we face will never compare to the suffering Jesus endured on the cross for our sake.

Christ voluntarily hung naked, soaked in His own blood as the Roman soldiers mocked and spit in His face. But as the crown of thorns sent drops of blood streaming down his face, He didn't say to Himself, "Just a little bit more suffering, and it'll all be over, and then I'll go down in history as an admired religious leader." Yeah, not quite!

The thing is, Jesus could have easily backed out. He was God's Son, after all. And yet He withheld the power that coursed through His veins. He resisted the temptation to call for angels to rescue Him and demolish the Roman soldiers. Why? Because another force, one far more potent than the nails that penetrated through His hands, held Him to the cross.

Love was the force. Not religion. This fuel strengthened Jesus to carry out His Father's perfect plan for His life.

And it can do the same with yours as well.

Running on Empty

I remember the first time I tried to pull an all-nighter. Notice the word *tried*. I was nine years old. My best friend was spending the night, and I don't know whose idea it was, but we thought, "Hey, if we stay up all night, then we'd have more time to play!"

So that's what we did—or, at least, that's what we *attempted* to do. But we could only watch so many movies and play so many games until the slumber crept in and sucked away our fun at six in the morning. We didn't *want* to give in, of course. We wanted to keep trying to create our own lotion concoctions. These concoctions were created by mixing a variety of different lotions. We were quite a creative duo. But we had spent all the energy stored in our little nine-year-old bodies.

And our bodies were begging for a refuel.

Have you ever attempted an all-nighter? Maybe you had an important exam to study for and needed the extra hours to review material. If so, can you recall how it felt to take the test the next day? Perhaps your mind wasn't all there. Staying up all night probably made it nearly impossible to recall everything you had spent so long studying.

Our bodies were never wired to run on empty. We can only go so far—mentally, physically, and even spiritually—until we hit a wall.

I don't know what your dreams and ambitions are. Maybe you aspire to become a teacher, a doctor, an actress, or a politician. Perhaps you aren't quite sure yet. Whatever your future looks like, I believe God has already planned how He wants to use you. There's an assignment in your life only you can carry out. A role only you can fill.

Yes, this is a privilege—but it is also a responsibility.

Because we will never be able to accomplish our God-given purpose if we are running low on fuel.

Our bodies need to recover mentally and physically at night if we hope to experience all the possibilities of the next day; in the same way, our hearts need a daily renewing and replenishing of God's presence if we hope to be used to our fullest potential.

Otherwise, our work is only going to leave us drained.

Otherwise, we may end up living for God through our good works alone rather than by the devotion of our hearts.

This is when Christianity becomes a religion rather than a relationship.

If we go throughout an entire day without drinking

water, what happens? We dehydrate. Run out of energy. Can't think straight. In the same way, God's Word is Living Water (see John 4:10–14), and it is far more sustaining to our souls than even natural water is to our bodies.

So how can we keep ourselves from running low on fuel? By spending daily time with God. Drinking from His Living Water of the Word. Refueling. Replenishing.

It is for our own benefit, after all!

Filled to Overflowing

Think about how you and your friends get to know each other better. By spending more time together, right? My friends and I like to get breakfast every now and then, and it's during that time we catch up. And the more time we hang out together, the more we discover new things about each other.

As you may already know, the same happens when we make it a priority to spend time with God. He longs for us to come and hang out with Him so we can get to know Him better. Fall deeper in love with Him.

But it's not easy, is it? Maybe your house is crazy in the mornings just like mine was when I was a teen. Maybe a thousand thoughts flood your mind the moment you wake up: *My hair needs to be straightened. Eggs need to be flipped. Oh, I completely forgot about that algebra assignment! And what am I going to wear?*

I get it. Life demands attention.

And that's exactly why I can no longer skip out on hydrating with God's Living Water each day—because being dehydrated is no fun. That's when I start running on empty and become too sluggish, cranky, and unmotivated to move forward.

But I need to stay replenished, because there's a yearning inside of me—a desire to live a life that outlasts this world. I want to be like a single ember that has the potential to ignite a fire. A wildfire that can spread throughout this world, even when I'm gone.

I don't want to be just another Christian who goes to church every week and reads her Bible occasionally. After all, last week's hydration has already worn off. Engaging with God was never meant to be just a once-a-week activity.

If you desire to live a life of meaning as well, I pray you will know the habits to form that can help you stay spiritually hydrated and empowered by God's Word.

I pray you will be filled to overflowing just as Ephesians 3:19 (TPT) speaks about: *"...this extravagant love pours into you until you are filled to overflowing with the fullness of God!"*

Because, you see, God has a journey for you to take. And everyone who has ever been on a road trip understands it's impossible to make it for the long haul without refueling.

Refueling with God is different, though, because He doesn't just give us barely enough. He gives us so much that we're overflowing into the lives of others. It's then we have what we need to carry out our assignments, as mentioned in Ephesians 3:20b (TPT): *"He will achieve infinitely more than your greatest request, your most unbelievable dream, and exceed your wildest imagination! He will outdo them all, for his miraculous power constantly energizes you."*

Constantly energizes you.

Sounds like some powerful fuel, wouldn't you agree?

Chapter Three
Behind the Steering Wheel

Most teenagers in the US attain their driver's permit and license as soon as they are of age.

Me?

I tried putting it off for as long as I possibly could.

I mean, there I was, a five-foot-zero fifteen-year-old, behind the wheel of a monstrous machine—one that kills lives every day—and I was in charge of navigating it. One wrong move could not just put my own life at risk, but the lives of others as well.

Who ever thought it was a good idea to give teenagers permission to start driving? I wanted to find that person and demand they increase the driving age by a few years at least. (True story. I even wrote an entire persuasive essay in school about how the driving age shouldn't be so young.)

Looking back, I can see how this fear of overseeing a vehicle reflected my fear of being in charge of my own life.

Perhaps being the baby of my family played a factor in this tendency to avoid independence, while most teens couldn't wait to test out their wings for the first time.

In case you're wondering, yes, I did grow out of this eventually. "Grow out of" may not be the correct term here. It was more like *force myself to get over it because that's life.*

But do you know what I never grew out of?

A *disgust* toward being independent.

Sure, it might look like I'm the only one behind the steering wheel of my life—navigating the roads and deciding whether I should turn left, right, or halt to a stop altogether. The truth is, I wouldn't have been able to steer my life even one inch without God's guidance.

You see, once we accept Christ, each of us are faced with a decision: Will we follow God's guidance as we navigate the unknown paths ahead of us? Or will we ask that He remain in the passenger seat and merely bless the choices we decide to make?

No More Wasted Time

There's a well-known rocker named Brian "Head" Welch whose itch to do life on his own terms compelled him to steer himself onto the road of fame, success, and pleasure. The band Korn was popular in the 90s and early 2000s, and their music changed the course of rock and metal music history.[4] Their songs—"devil music," as many Christians referred to them—quickly climbed the charts during those years.

During the primetime of their fame, Brian seemed to

have it all. He had paved his own road toward success and happiness. What more could he ask for?

To those who admired this band, they probably assumed he was navigating his life just fine on his own. No need for God when all seems to be riding smoothly in life, right?

But appearances were deceiving. Because even though Brian seemed to "have it all" on the outside, on the inside, he wanted to die. Pain burned inside of him like a blazing fire. He tried to extinguish this fire by using alcohol and drugs, but that lifestyle just fanned the flames into a wildfire. Eventually, that blaze consumed him to the point Brian believed nothing could be powerful enough to douse the agony and restore the damage caused by his destructive choices.

What did that damage look like, you ask? A divorce that left him as a single dad with an out-of-control addiction to drugs and alcohol.[5]

It was in this all-hope-is-lost moment when Brian reached out for a savior and cried out to God, in hopes that God could pull him out of the fire that had swept over his life.

After a friend invited Brian to church, he started reading the Bible for himself, and an amazing thing happened: God showered Brian with affection. Brian claims the love that poured inside of him in that moment completely took over his earthly desire to get high on drugs.

Those harsh flames vanished within an instant.

That love and grace was strong enough not only to extinguish the fire, but to bring recompense for the destruction it had caused in his life.

Knowing God became all that mattered to Brian from that point on. He threw away his drugs, no longer needing the high they offered. Nor did he need the satisfaction of wealth and fame, so he decided to split from the band.[6]

Brian wanted God to take the steering wheel of his life from that point on. The thrill that had originally come from being in the driver's seat of his life had long worn off and wasn't what he had expected. So from then on, Brian not only wanted Jesus Christ to be His Savior, but he wanted to release control over his decisions so he could live in God's perfect will.

Even if that meant leaving behind his rockstar lifestyle.

Brian was once asked in an interview why he believes God put him on this earth. Take a look at his response:

He put me on earth to have fellowship and intimacy with Him. And I'm going to spend as much time as I possibly can getting to know him every day. I don't want to waste any time. I've wasted enough time. That's what I'm put on earth to do: be intimate with God, get to know Him as much as I can, let Him fill me with His spirit, so that He can do the work by bringing people into the Kingdom.[7]

No Shame in God-Dependence

Maybe you're like me and you've never had a desire to live the rockstar lifestyle Brian once had. Still, there's no denying our American culture praises those who forge their own path to success and happiness. Because that's what the

American Dream is, right? That explains why shows like *Shark Tank* are so popular. It's inspiring to be reminded we can create a successful life. One we love. There are no limits. Anything is possible if we are strong-willed and independent enough to pursue it.

Of course, it's not evil to be passionate about our lives. (Or to watch the show *Shark Tank*. It's one of my favorites, actually!) But we must admit this kind of thinking has shaped our society into one that has a constant pressure to *be perfect.*

Maintain straight-A grades so you can receive a scholarship. Train harder to be accepted onto that college basketball team. Aim high in life. The ball is in your court, after all! (*Cringe.* Puns not intended.)

And since we're the ones supposedly "in control," then it's our fault if we miss the mark. Am I right? Or if we can't aim high enough without asking for assistance—because some of us weren't blessed with the gift of height (*raises hand*)—then we feel like we're weak. Incapable. Something must be wrong with us.

How sad is that? It's the complete opposite of what we are told in Scripture. Instead of being ashamed of our weaknesses, it can be freeing to *rejoice* in them. That is what Paul meant when he wrote 2 Corinthians 12:9–11:

> *Each time he said, "My grace is all you need. My power works best in weakness." So now I am glad to boast about my weaknesses, so that the power of Christ can work through me. That's why I take pleasure in my weaknesses, and in the insults, hardships, persecutions, and troubles that I suffer for Christ. For when I am weak, then I am strong.*

Truth is, *God never intended us to live with an independent mentality that separates us from His presence.* He invites us to do life *with* Him. Not just on Sundays. He wants us to be God-dependent on Him every day.

We simply *can't* do life on our own. Nor can we create a life that ushers in perfect wealth, happiness, success, and abundance.

What a freeing thought!

When I acknowledge *I am only human,* pressure dissolves. The weight that had once crushed me, suffocating me from life, finally lifts, enabling me to take a deep breath. *Whew.*

There's no shame in admitting our shortcomings. It's liberating, actually, to scoot out of the driver's seat and invite God to take the lead.

Because regardless of what many of us believe, we were simply never created to do life apart from Him. We were never created to live with this independent, I-can-do-it-all mentality.

It's only in admitting these weaknesses that we can finally learn to become *God*-dependent.

Passenger or Driver's Seat?

Confession: There are still times today, ten years after attaining my driver's license, that my hands tremble behind a steering wheel. I grew up in a small(ish) town in South Carolina, so traffic-packed roads can produce a bead of sweat on my forehead sometimes. If only you could've witnessed when I had to navigate the Atlanta highways by myself for the first time! If you're looking for a way to increase your heart rate without doing cardio, consider giving that one a try.

Yes, driving can still be daunting at times.

Yes, navigating life—making adultish decisions—can be terrifying. I won't try to soften the blow for you. As a teenager, I'm sure you're already aware those choices you make now are crucial in determining your course ahead.

But there's good news! We don't need to study the map before we take off on the journey. We don't need to know every twist and turn along the way. *We only need to know the One whose hands guide ours.* The One who has already divinely designed the map of our lives.

God doesn't *want* to abandon us to embark on life's path solo. This is made evident in the passage of Proverbs 3:5–6 (TPT):

> *Trust in the Lord completely,*
> *and do not rely on your own opinions.*
> *With all your heart rely on him to guide you,*
> *and he will lead you in every decision you make.*
> *Become intimate with him in whatever you do,*
> *and he will lead you wherever you go.*

I don't know about you, but I can breathe a little easier after reading that. Because at last, I can relinquish control. At last, we can forsake our tendencies to strive hard in our own efforts. And when we do finally scoot over and allow our Heavenly Father to be our navigator, our racing heartbeat will cease. Merely knowing—*trusting*—that He is our guide fills us with a sense of peace. The only kind of peace powerful enough to still our trembling hands.

Now the question I want to leave you with is this:

Is God in the passenger seat or driver's seat of your life?

If He's in the driver's seat, then fasten your seatbelt. You're going to be in for quite the adventure!

Review

- We were created for intimacy with our Heavenly Father. It's out of this love relationship with Him that we discover who we are, why we're on earth, and our life's purpose.

- It's God's love, not religion, that will fuel us to live a life of meaning and impact.

- The only way we can live according to our true purpose is by allowing God to direct our steps, living according to His will rather than our own.

Replenish

"God showed how much he loved us by sending his one and only Son into the world so that we might have eternal life through him" (1 John 4:9).

"For this is how God loved the world: He gave his one and only Son, so that everyone who believes in him will not perish but have eternal life" (John 3:16).

"We have come into an intimate experience with God's love, and we trust in the love he has for us. God is love! Those who are living in love are living in God, and God lives through them" (1 John 4:16, TPT).

"Then you will be empowered to discover what every holy one experiences—the great magnitude of the astonishing love of Christ in all its dimensions. How deeply intimate and far-reaching is his love! How enduring and inclusive it is! Endless love beyond measurement that transcends our understanding—this extravagant love pours into you until you are filled to overflowing with the fullness of God! Never doubt God's mighty power to work in you and accomplish all this. He will achieve infinitely more than your greatest request, your most unbelievable dream, and exceed your wildest imagination! He will outdo them all, for his miraculous power constantly energizes you" (Ephesians 3:18–20, TPT).

"Trust in the Lord completely,
and do not rely on your own opinions.
  With all your heart rely on him to guide you,
    and he will lead you in every decision you make.
Become intimate with him in whatever you do,
  and he will lead you wherever you go"
(Proverbs 3:5–6, TPT).

Respond
Influencer Challenge

Use your sphere of influence on social media by sparking a discussion about this chapter with your friends. I challenge you to write a post that answers the following question. Be sure to use the hashtag #BecomeAnInfluencer in your response.

If you aren't on social media, no worries! You can participate in the same challenge among your friends in real life.

In what ways will receiving God's love empower you to spread His light, attract others to Him, and help you to carry out your assignment in His kingdom?

Part Two
Embracing Your Unique Position

Chapter Four
Is it Selfish to Love Yourself?

I attended a one-year-old's birthday party the other day. This little girl is the cutest toddler I've ever met: She has a fine layer of bleached-blond hair and ocean blue eyes, squeezable cheeks, and kissable lips. Any time she hears music playing, she can't help but move along to the beat. This one-year-old loves to blow kisses, wave at strangers, splash around in the ocean with her daddy, dance to songs from Disney movies, and FaceTime with family. And she gives high-pitched squeals every time she sees a dog.

If you haven't caught on yet, this one-year-old is pretty much perfect in every way.

But I might be a little biased. Because she is none other than my one-and-only niece, Nusa.

I often wonder—do other people view her the same way? Or is my perspective influenced by a love strong enough to look past the flaws? Like the times when she fusses or has a blow-out in her diaper, or well, I've run out of imperfections to list for her!

You see, the love I have for my niece highlights her beauty.

This is how it typically is with parental love. Am I right? True love lasers in on the beauty, emphasizing it so much that the flaws fade into the background.

If a baby who is loved in this way can grow up to view themselves through the eyes of this parental love, they'd be less likely to develop insecurity issues. Don't you think?

In the same way, I wonder if our insecurity issues would dissolve if we, too, learned to view ourselves through the lenses of God's parental love. If we could shake off the web of insecurities that have entangled us for so long, can you imagine the freedom? Then, when God calls us to take a bold leap of faith, we wouldn't give the excuse "I don't have what it takes." Instead, we'd have the necessary confidence to fulfill our God-given assignments with boldness.

But is it selfish of us, as Christians, to learn to love ourselves like Jesus does? And how will overcoming insecurity issues better prepare our hearts to love others?

Suffocated by Shame

Kids roamed the middle school hallways. I kept my head down, staring at my shoes as I shuffled to lunch. Chatter and laughter bounced off the walls, and my back ached beneath the weight of my heavy backpack. It would be another day of lugging around my textbooks simply because I was too ashamed to admit that I didn't understand how to unlock my locker.

In the cafeteria, I sat with the same group of girls every day. I'd become friends with these girls in elementary school. But this was sixth grade, not fifth—and although there was only a year of difference between the two grades, it was as if we'd jumped over middle school and landed in high school. I hardly spoke a word as they gossiped, talked about boys, and showed off pieces from their new wardrobes.

How had I become the odd-one-out? I had plenty of friends in elementary school. But now it was as though a sense of shame had slithered around my neck, choking me, constricting my ability to speak even one word. I truly felt as though people were staring at me in school. Like they were laughing internally, as if I were an amusing sight for them to behold.

It seemed like an eternity had passed by the time my mom finally picked me up from school. As soon as I lowered into the passenger seat, I released the built-up tears. "I haven't talked to a single person all day," I remember telling her. Over time, I'd try and convince her to pull me out and homeschool me. "I feel like I'm suffocating when I'm at school."

Suffocating.

Somehow, that snake of self-shame had coiled around my neck, cutting off my oxygen supply. It wasn't that people were *actually* staring at me, or laughing internally, or thinking I was weird. Yet even if they were, that wasn't the root of the issue.

The only reason I was miserable that year was because I'd allowed myself to believe the lies. That I wasn't good enough. That I was different from those other girls, so why even bother trying to make friends? I wasn't as attractive as them, so might as well lower my head so they won't look at me. I wasn't as outgoing, so if I kept my mouth shut then I wouldn't embarrass myself.

Suffocation is the opposite of *freedom*.

Suffocation keeps us from relishing in the life Christ died for.

Looking back, I can't help but wonder what if I'd learned to define myself through Jesus' words rather than my own? What if I'd worn an invisible name tag that said "loved" and "accepted" and "redeemed" rather than the labels I thought others had placed on me?

I'll tell you what would've happened: That love would've crushed the neck of that life-sucking serpent (see Genesis 3:14–15). I would've finally been free to gasp for fresh air. No longer would I be concerned about what others were thinking of me, because I would've known my identity wasn't found in their opinions but in *my Father's* truth.

And with my head risen with confidence instead of lowered in shame, perhaps I would've been more attentive to the needs of those around me. Those who needed the light of Christ that radiated from within me.

The Selfishness of Insecurity

I may not know who you are, but I strongly believe God wants to use you. And I'm not referring to some faraway future when you're my age or older. I'm talking about right now. Today, not tomorrow.

But, you see, insecurity is a thief. It prevents us from allowing God to use us. It trains us to focus on ourselves alone, planting voices in our mind that sound like this:

Does this outfit make me look fat?

Gosh, I hate the sound of my voice.

Why can't I look like that influencer on Instagram?

No, loving ourselves is not selfish. It's the opposite.

Being *insecure* in ourselves is selfish. Because if our gaze is centered on nitpicking our every flaw, then how will we look up in time to see the girl God wants us to talk to in the cafeteria? If we're too embarrassed by the sound of our own voice, does that mean we're going to remain silent when we need to speak up and share the gospel?

There's a reason the Enemy continues his attempts at defeating Christians with insecurity. He knows it'll keep us paralyzed. Immobile. Unwilling to carry out our assignments because we're too afraid of how we'll appear to others. John 10:10a tells us *"the thief's purpose is to steal and kill and destroy."* He has one goal in mind: To thwart God's kingdom from advancing.

Have you ever been choked by the same serpent of self-shame like I was in sixth grade? If so, in what ways did that prevent you from sharing your light for Christ?

Perhaps it's time we silence the Enemy rather than vice versa. It's time we allow God's cleansing love to wash over our eyes and grant us renewed sight. To restore the perception we have of ourselves in our reflections. How can we do this?

Let's remember the truth found in 2 Timothy 1:7: *"For God has not given us a spirit of fear and timidity, but of power, love, and self-discipline."*

Fear of men is not from God.

Timidity is not from God.

Rather, God's *"perfect love expels all fear"* (1 John 4:18). God's love is like a disinfectant that expels the fear of people and their opinions. It drives out our fear of embarrassing ourselves, of failing, of not measuring up.

This love breaks the paralyzing grip of insecurity and grants us the freedom we need to take bold steps of confidence as we carry out our assignments.

It's true this world is filled with confident, self-loving people. These people are unashamed to speak up and use their voices—but many of them are influencing the world in ways that go against God's Word. What would happen, though, if those of us who are in Christ took the stage instead? What would happen if we reclaimed our spot behind the microphone and influenced this world for God rather than for evil?

We first must relent in complaining about the sound of our voice and instead use the instruments we've been given to influence this world for Jesus. This life is far too short to live it with our eyes focused on ourselves alone.

Running to Win

I chuckle a little when I recall how self-conscious I was back in sixth grade—so much that I refused to use my locker. I would've rather lived with the back pain caused by a heavy backpack instead of the pain of self-shame. How ridiculous of me! That insecurity created an unnecessary weight that I lugged around every single day.

Literally and figuratively.

Has insecurity created unnecessary burdens for you as well? If so, I encourage you to drop the weight at the foot of the cross. One of the reasons Jesus died was so we could be free to live without baggage. So why should we cling to it, lug it around until we develop back issues, when Jesus has already transferred it onto Himself when He hung on the cross?

Hebrews 12:1 says, *"Therefore, since we are surrounded by such a huge crowd of witnesses to the life of faith, let us strip off every weight that slows us down, especially the sin that so easily trips us up. And let us run with endurance the race God has set before us."*

You have been placed on this earth at this time in history so you can make an impact no one else can. God has set before you a race that only you can run. That'll be quite the challenge to "run with endurance" if you're hobbling along, a weight of insecurity crushing your back and keeping you from giving it your all, don't you think?

I encourage you to surrender this weight to Jesus. No longer does it need to hold you back. Allow God's love to enable you to view yourself the way He sees you. If you do this, nothing will be strong enough to keep you from striding toward the finish line, winning the race you have been called to run.

Chapter Five
Royal Identity

Imagine this: One day, you're going about your daily business—maybe you just returned home from soccer practice and you're dripping with sweat, about to hop in the shower—and you receive a phone call from a stranger with some life-altering news. This can't possibly be true. It must be a prank call. You can't even respond at first because your mouth hangs wide open.

But it's legit.

Your birth parents are royalty. That means you are royalty as well.

How could that be? You've lived your entire life as any other normal person. You grew up in a normal family just like everyone else you know. It'd require some major brain rewiring to accept this new fact, don't you think? (Perhaps that's why Mia Thermopolis had such a hard time doing just that in the movie *The Princess Diaries!*)

This may sound far-fetched, but it happened IRL to an American-raised woman named Sarah Culberson. At the age of twenty-eight, after searching for her birth parents, she received a phone call from her birth uncle who gave her this life-altering news.

Her father was a Paramount Chief, which meant that she was a princess in a West African country.[8]

Sarah fully embraced her new status as a royal, as well as the responsibilities that came along with it—even though it meant forsaking her former life as an actress and dancer.[9]

But what would've happened if she'd refused to accept this new role? What if she never allowed her life to become altered by this newfound reality, and instead she continued with her daily business?

How sad would that be! After all, her role as a princess has since given her the opportunity to restore damage caused by war in her birth family's tribe. Her mere presence has offered hope and a helping hand to these people. Sarah would not be making the difference she's making now if she never stepped into her royal identity.

Sadly, there are many Christians who are still neglecting their calling, their true God-given potential, because they never allowed themselves to become transformed by this new identity. These people may go about their daily business as usual, believing they are nobody. Acting as though they never experienced a life-changing moment when they accepted Jesus Christ into their hearts.

We have been called to perform "royal duties" while on this earth. But we can't do this if we never allow our confidence and our lives to become defined by our identity in

Christ. So if we hope to make an eternal difference, we must first answer the question: What does it mean to be a new person in Jesus Christ—a child of the King of Kings?

A Royal Celebration

Sarah's new position as a princess called for a royal celebration among the Bumpe community. How crazy it must have been for Sarah to see the hundreds of people who welcomed her and celebrated her arrival! People danced throughout the village. The women sang, "We are preparing for Sarah." Even the children were elated to welcome this new princess. Sarah, of course, couldn't show up for this celebration wearing everyday attire; instead, her biological father gave her a beautiful green gown, truly befitting for royalty of their tribe.[10]

She was officially a princess.

When describing this event, Sarah said, "It was a life-altering experience...shocking, amazing, overwhelming, exciting. It was beautiful, glorious and uplifting!"[11]

You know what's really cool? When we accept Jesus into our hearts, we receive our own "welcome party" as well. This is made evident in Luke 15:10 (TPT): *"[God] says to all his angels, 'Let's have a joyous celebration, for the one who was lost, I have found!'"*

How silly would it be for us to experience this transition—*shocking, beautiful,* and *glorious,* to use Sarah's adjectives—and remain unchanged? 2 Corinthians 5:17 tells us *"anyone who belongs to Christ has become a new person. The old life is gone; a new life has begun!"*

A new life. A new person.

That truly is a reason to celebrate! We can hold our heads up high because we are no longer defined by our past. Jesus has provided us with a clean slate. Our life is changed for all eternity!

And in this new identity and life comes new responsibilities. We now have a greater role to play—an important calling to step into.

This calling isn't a burden, you see; it's an honor.

Listen to how Sarah describes her new life and position as a royal:

"And it's [life] changed it for the better," she said. ". . . I see I'm just one of the moving parts in the work being done in Sierra Leone. I honor it and I cherish it."[12]

In the same way, each one of us are a moving part in the work being done in the kingdom of God. And there is a *lot* of work to be done. But we can't do this work—perform our royal duties—until we first allow our source of confidence to be rooted in our royal identity in Christ.

An Attractive Confidence

While watching a video of Sarah in an interview, I couldn't help but notice how she radiates with confidence. Notice that I didn't say *arrogance.* Her mannerisms, the way she handles herself and responds to questions, don't come across as though she were thinking, "Gosh, I am just *so amazing."* After all, she couldn't have attained this royal status with her own intelligence, skills, or looks. It was a status she was born into. And in this status, she has a reason to portray humble confidence. (No, that is not an oxymoron.)

This confidence empowers Sarah to make a difference.

In the same way, we have not done anything to earn our position in Christ, so there's nothing we can do to tamper our identity in Him either. When we finally allow ourselves to become defined by who God says we are, then we will be empowered with confidence. An air of self-assurance that enables us to carry out our assignments.

So how can we allow ourselves to be defined by this identity? To answer this question, I want to share a glimpse of how my life looked before I developed a relationship with Jesus:

Christianity was a religion for me. Insecurity kept me shriveled in my shell, hiding the light of Christ within me. But as I fell more in love with Jesus—as I spent time devouring the Bible on my own—that's when that shell began to crack. Little by little. I stopped believing the lies that something was wrong with me because I knew I was created in the image of God (Genesis 1:27). I stopped comparing myself to others because my desire had now become to look like *Christ* rather than men.

Soon, my light burst out of the dark shell that had once kept me hidden. Finally exposed, I've been free to be *"the light of the world—like a city on a hilltop that cannot be hidden"* (Matthew 5:14).

If you long to break free from your shell—to be empowered with confidence to make an eternal difference—take a moment to consider how the Bible defines your identity.

As a new creation in Jesus, you are . . .

- Designed in the womb, wonderfully made, and never out of God's mind or sight (Psalms 139:13–18).

- God's handiwork, created to do good works (Ephesians 2:10).

- Chosen before the creation of the world and appointed (Ephesians 1:4, John 15:16).

- A child of God (John 1:12).

- Adopted into God's family (Ephesians 1:5).

- The work of God's hands (Isaiah 64:8).

- Never separated from God's love (Romans 8:35–39).

- No longer condemned by your past failures (Romans 8:1).

- Created by God and redeemed (Isaiah 43:1).

- Heirs of God and co-heirs with Christ (Romans 8:17).

Have you ever noticed how earthly royals carry an elegant air about them? The way they speak, act, dress, interact with others. All of this is influenced by their status as a royal. Why, then, should it be any different for those of us who have been adopted into the royal family of Jesus Christ? Everyone we interact with should sense we are different. Our presence—the outpouring of God's love from within us—should brighten the atmosphere. We don't walk with our heads lowered. We don't play comparison games on social media, pushing others down so we can lift ourselves higher. Instead, we are the young women who radiate with the confidence of Christ as His light shines from within.

That is the attractive kind of confidence I aspire to have. What about you?

"Do You Know Who You Are?"

When Sarah's birth uncle called to deliver this life-altering news to her, he said, "We are so happy you've been found. Do you know who you are?"[13]

Does that not give you chills? Those of us in Christ know what it's like to be found. As soon as we accepted Christ as our Savior, He rejoiced from His position in heaven.

And now I ask you the same question Sarah's uncle asked her:

Do you know who you are?

Do you know how valuable and beautiful and precious you are in His sight? How loved you are? If not, take a moment to consider the cross. Reflect on the tremendous price Jesus paid to restore your place in the family of God. He didn't just *tell* us how much He loved us—although He could have. But what is love without action? Jesus displayed this love for us when He voluntarily suffered and died a criminal's death on the cross, exchanging His life for ours.

And that, my friend, is how loved you are in His sight.

Do you know who you are? Have you truly grasped this? Not just with your mind, but with your heart? Have you allowed this royal identity to penetrate deep within you, so much it affects everything you do and say and your self-perception?

In a video on Sarah's website, she said she couldn't just return to the US after seeing the condition of the Bumpe village in Africa. "This is my family, and we've gotta do something."[14]

In the same way, our royal status isn't merely for our own enjoyment. We weren't meant to keep these privileges all to ourselves. Rather, our royal duties involve bringing as many people into this kingdom as possible. We can't carry on with our lives, ignoring the responsibility we have as daughters of Christ. We can't just look at the condition of this unsaved world and say, "Oh, well. I hope they figure it out somehow."

Time is ticking. People are lost. Searching. Desperate. Headed for eternal destruction.

They need to hear the Good News just like we did before we met Jesus.

Will you be the one who delivers this Good News to them? Will you be confident enough to share about the royal position they've been invited to accept in Jesus Christ?

Chapter Six
Your Unique Impact

There's a common misconception that, if you want to become a movie star, then you must be jaw-droppingly gorgeous and have a great figure or you don't even have a chance. But that's not necessarily the case. As I've worked on film projects throughout the years, I've been taught a theory to debunk that myth:

Embrace what makes you different with all you've got. Because casting directors aren't looking for cookie cutter performers. They're searching for real people to portray real people on the screen.

This means, if there's something distinctive about your appearance or personality, a trait that sets you apart, don't hide it. Use it to your advantage. Because there won't be any other actor in that audition who has those same traits.

In fact, those unique qualities can help you stand out and be more memorable to the casting directors. And what actor *doesn't* hope to leave a lasting impression on a casting director?

For example—when the actress Julia Roberts was in her teen years, she was ashamed of her big mouth and full lips. Now, however, she appreciates it, because she knows her smile helps set her apart from other actresses.[15]

Another thespian who comes to mind is Vanessa Paradis. She's a French singer, model, and actress who is unashamed of the large gap between her two front teeth. Why try to hide the gap when it only contributes to her beauty?

Perhaps you're not an actress, but you may be tempted at times to hide what makes you unique. And I'm not referring to appearance qualities alone. If you've struggled with comparing yourself to another girl—striving to become more like *her*—why? Do you feel like you're not enough the way God created you?

This principle I've learned in acting applies to real life as well. We aren't meant to be cookie cutter copies of each other. How boring would that be! Rather, God created each of us in a distinct manner. And these unique qualities can help us further our assigned role in God's kingdom. In other words, it is *our uniqueness that qualifies us to live out our destined purpose.*

So what does this journey of embracing these traits look like, and how will doing so help to further your calling as influencer?

The Art of Embracing

Japanese culture understands the art of embracing unique qualities and imperfections. When a piece of pottery breaks—such as a mug or a pot—most people would toss it out or attempt to glue the ceramic pieces back together. But not the Japanese. They use a method known as the Kintsugi technique that can increase both the value and the beauty of a broken piece of pottery.

Rather than trying to hide the cracks in the artifact, this method *highlights* them by using lacquer, a special kind of smooth coating, and dusts the cracks with powdered gold. The result is an eye-catching, revamped piece of pottery as the golden seams glint where the cracks and chips once were.[16]

These pieces of art are stunning. If you have a chance, take a moment to Google this type of pottery so you can see them for yourself. (Try not to go down a rabbit hole though.)

Isn't it cool to see how these fractures and imperfections can become *enhanced* rather than hidden? I can't imagine what this world would look like if we all did the same with our unique qualities as well. Rather than trying to blend in and be like everyone else, we could instead embrace those things that can make us beautiful, those qualities that could leave an impression on everyone we meet. Those traits could be the very aspects that allure people to us, catching their attention and giving us an opportunity to make an impact.

Jesus' light shines on the inside of us. Our unique traits can serve a purpose in exposing His light in a special way. For example, do you have a bubbly personality? Embrace it! God's joy can radiate from your smile. Are you passionate about science or math? That's awesome. What a great opportunity to emphasize His intelligence and design in all creation and reach people in a way in which I am unqualified. (Well, unqualified and *unpassionate.* Which isn't a word, but still. Huge props to those of you who are into math and science!)

Those golden seams created by the Kintsugi technique are the very qualities that attract people's attention. Those one-of-a-kind mugs and vases lure shoppers into buying them.

What if, by allowing Jesus' light to burst forth from inside of our "cracks" and distinctive qualities, we could tap into our unique potential to reach people? To invite them into knowing the source inside of us?

We can't afford to keep ourselves hidden. If we did, then we'd forsake the unique ways in which God longs to radiate from inside of us and set this world ablaze for His kingdom!

Uncovering Our Purpose

Embracing our unique qualities is part of the journey we take toward discovering our God-given purpose. Once we have rooted our identity in who we are in Christ, then we can uncover those unique traits and skills God wants us to use in our position as influencer.

To give you an example—I grew up as the youngest kid in a family of three girls, as well as the youngest of thirteen cousins. As you can imagine, our family gatherings were pretty crazy, especially since most of my cousins are female. And, well, we all know how us girls like to talk. Except I was one of the quieter ones. Although I could have stayed quiet because of how difficult it was to be heard among such a noisy family. Anyway, over time, I began to view my introverted personality and quiet voice as a crack. A flaw to be ashamed of, and one that needed to be hidden out of sight of anyone who could tease me, because I wasn't like the other girls who were loud, crazy, and had extroverted personalities.

I believed the lie that said I needed to blend in with everyone else.

As I drew closer to Christ and discovered my identity in Him, I broke free from this self-shame and learned how to embrace these qualities.

My introverted personality I once thought was an imperfection has helped me further my calling as a writer. My personality allows me to be an observer in social settings. I can have the patience I need to sit for long periods of time and write.

Along with this personality comes other traits as well. I took the Myers-Brigg Type Indicator® personality test and discovered I am an INFP—introverted, sensitive, empathetic, and imaginative. How cool to witness how each of these traits serves a purpose in my calling! If I resented this personality and never allowed it to influence my writing, speaking, and acting, then I wouldn't have developed the potential God has given me to bless people in a unique way.

What characteristics and qualities has God gifted you? Consider taking a moment to list all that come to mind—including those you may have disregarded in the past. Then, take a look at this list and consider how these qualities can be used to expose the light of Christ. If you have permission from your parents, you may want to take the Myers-Brigg Type Indicator® personality test to take a deeper look at your potential personality strengths. Ask God how He would like you to use these facets to help you carry out your calling—the special ways He has ordained you to bless the world around you.

Free to Shine

"What is it you can bring to the role no one else can?" Actors often hear this question from their acting coaches. And now I want to ask you the same question.

What can you offer this world that no one else can?

We know, from Psalm 139:14, we have been created "wonderfully complex" by our Creator. Verse sixteen goes on to say, *"Every day of my life was recorded in your book."* If He has crafted us with such skill and intention, don't you know our unique design has a purpose? One that can help us fulfill the story He has written in His book?

As you learn to embrace this unique role—this "wonderfully complex" design of yours—don't be surprised if you find the weight of insecurity lifting from your shoulders. Don't be surprised if that nagging voice becomes silenced, the one that once said you needed to be prettier. Different. Skinnier. Or that there were imperfections that needed to be photoshopped away.

God's piercing light of love will melt away that added pressure of insecurity, leaving you feeling lighter, more joyful, and overall, *freer* to be who God has designed you to be.

This is the same freedom I enjoyed when I first discovered, as an actress, that I didn't need to compare myself to other actresses. I was free to embrace. Free to focus on what I could bring to the role that no one else could. *That was when I truly found more joy in acting. When I became free to shine.*

No more comparison, striving, or hiding.

It's like the Kintsugi technique in pottery. We don't need to toss ourselves aside because we feel like we're broken with imperfections. Nor do we need to struggle, attempting to glue the pieces together, simply so we can look like everyone else. Why go through the trouble when there is beauty to be poured out in the art of embracing?

We are free to shine. No, let me rephrase that: We are free to accept those aspects about ourselves that set us apart. Because those things that appear to be cracks may not be flaws at all; rather, they are indentations God has grafted upon us for a purpose. We weren't created to shine so that others could be attracted to us but so they could be attracted to the godly love *within us.* A love perfectly illuminated through these unique indentations.

Review

- We can overcome insecurity by allowing God's love to expel the fear of others. When this fear has vanished, we can then focus on pleasing God first by loving Him and loving others.

- If we hope to perform our duties as an influencer for God's kingdom, we must first accept our "royal identity" and allow this to transform everything we think, do, and say.

- As we learn to embrace our unique traits, personalities, and skills, we will discover how they can
be used to shine the light of Christ into the lives
of others.

Replenish

"Therefore, since we are surrounded by such a huge crowd of
witnesses to the life of faith, let us strip off every weight that
slows us down, especially the sin that so easily trips us up.
And let us run with endurance the race God has set before
us" (Hebrews 12:1).

"This means that anyone who belongs to Christ has become
a new person. The old life is gone; a new life has begun!" (2
Corinthians 5:17).

"The thief's purpose is to steal and kill and destroy. My purpose is to give them a rich and satisfying life" (John 10:10).

"You are the light of the world—like a city on a hilltop that
cannot be hidden" (Matthew 5:14).

"You made all the delicate, inner parts of my body
    and knit me together in my mother's womb.
Thank you for making me so wonderfully complex!
    Your workmanship is marvelous—how well I know it"
(Psalms 139:13–14).

Respond
Influencer Challenge

Use your sphere of influence on social media by sparking a discussion about this chapter with your friends! I challenge you to write a post that answers the following question. Be sure to use the hashtag #BecomeAnInfluencer in your response!

If you aren't on social media, no worries! You can participate in the same challenge among your friends in real life.

How could insecurity immobilize us from having the confidence we need to embrace our calling?

Part Three

Discovering and Developing Your Gifts

Chapter Seven
The Impact Zone

The other day, I came across a page in my journal I wrote as a kid. On this page I described what I wanted to do when I "grew up": Write and act. But I *especially* wanted to write.

No surprise there.

Twenty years later, writing and acting both play a role in my career. Writing, however, has always been my number one. It'd be so cool if I could show a glimpse of what my life looks like today to that eight-year-old me. I'd pull back the curtain where she could see me, right now, writing this book. Or maybe I'd give her a sneak peek of the virtual screening I attended last week for a short film I was in or even the writing workshop I taught for teens last Saturday.

I wouldn't share this with my eight-year-old self in hopes she would swell with pride over what I've done (trust me, my life truly isn't that glamorous!). Rather, I'd do this so she could swell with *faith* in God, trusting He's given her those dreams for a reason: To point her in the right direction for her life. And to encourage her to keep pursuing those God-given dreams.

Okay, I'll stop referring to my past self in third person now.

But sometimes I wonder …what if I'd never trusted that God placed these dreams on my heart for a reason? What if I didn't believe He gave these gifts to me so I could influence His kingdom?

I probably would've chosen a more stable career path. One that merely paid the bills but never gave me a chance to cultivate my strengths or devote my potential to further the Body of Christ.

Wouldn't it be awesome if all of us received a glimpse of our future when we were kids? That certainly would come in handy in your life right about now, don't you think? Yet even though God may not give you this sneak peek, He can still guide you on to the right path.

One way you can discover this path is by tapping into your "sweet spot." This is a term I first heard used by John Maxwell, and he refers to it as the place of "intersection of your success and someone else's" and "Using what you are best at to add value to others."[17] I like to refer to this as the "impact zone"—the place where we excel in our strengths, move toward our God-given dreams, and use our gifts to influence others for Christ.

So is it possible for you to venture onto a career path you are both passionate about and allows you to impact souls for eternity? And how can you embrace this impact zone?

From Violent Hands to Helping Hands

There once was a little boy, raised by a single mother, who grew up in poverty in the inner cites of Boston and Detroit. The violence that surrounded him in this environment caused him to display little effort in school. His report cards weren't worthy of hanging on the refrigerator door, to say the least. In fact, many students nicknamed him as "Dummy."[18] No wonder he didn't believe that he could excel in school with that kind of label.

Poor grades weren't his only struggle either. The inner turmoil this boy faced often erupted into fits of outrage at home. His pathological temper spiraled out of control, clinging to him like a disease he couldn't overcome, and this disease eventually led him to nearly kill his mother and a friend on two separate occasions. But before any damage could be done, God kept him from following through with these violent acts.

It wasn't until the last violent incident, when the boiling anger within cooled to a simmer, the teen's eyes were opened. He realized how the disease of rage had nearly stolen any potential to create a stable future for himself. In that moment, he cried out to God, knowing only God could heal him from this sickness of destructive anger issues.

Guess what happened? This teen never again allowed anger to reach a boiling point and explode into a violent act. From then on, he overcame the labels and strove harder in school. He broke free from the strongholds that had once warped his mind by his harsh environment, the lies that said he couldn't create a good future for himself. He instead believed God had called him to a greater purpose. This is what spurred him to pursue his dream to become a doctor. To use his hands to help others.[19]

That is exactly what he did. Not only did he become the best student in his class and in his school, but he also landed a scholarship to Yale University and then went on to medical school. By the time he was thirty-three, he became the youngest director of pediatric neurosurgery at the Johns Hopkins Hospital. One of his major accomplishments involved being the first to successfully separate Siamese twins.[20]

Who is this boy who transformed from violent hands to helping hands, from "Dummy" to "Doctor"? You may have heard of him when he ran in the Republican race for the 2016 presidential election. Ben Carson's story inspires millions as he continues to use his gifts to illuminate God's light into this dark world.

None of these successes would have occurred, however, if he did not strive to excel in his strengths, believing he could be used for a greater purpose.

In his book *Gifted Hands,* Ben Carson writes, "For whatever reason, the God of the universe, the God who holds galaxies in His hands, had seen a reason to reach down to a campus room on Planet Earth and send a dream to a discouraged ghetto kid who wanted to become a doctor."[21]

What was the purpose of this God-given dream? So he could be led onto the path he was meant to walk.

I can't help but wonder—what would've happened if he had continued to view himself as below-average? What if he had allowed the miserable environment of poverty and violence to mold his identity and future rather than God's Word? How tragic that would've been! Countless children would never have been given a second chance at life from the surgeries he's performed.

Ben Carson seemed to understand the power of this impact zone—the intersection of strength and influence. Sure, he could've settled for an easier route. A job that merely paid the bills would've been enough for him to survive.

But he didn't want to just survive. He wanted to *impact*. To unleash his strengths, trusting that, if God had placed that dream on his heart, then He could help him carry it through.

Embracing the Greatest Opportunity for Impact

I've never set foot on a surfboard before, but I am familiar with what is known as the impact zone. According to TheFreeDictionary.com, this is the "spot on a wave where the water is just about to collapse and explode, entailing the greatest opportunity and danger for a surfer."[22]

The greatest opportunity and the greatest potential for danger.

If each of us listened to our God-given dreams and found careers that allowed us to use these impact zones, there's no telling the potential we could have for influence! But it's scary, isn't it? I get it. The wave of your God-given dream may appear massive. The idea of actually allowing the surge of water to swoop you up can be daunting. What about the possible injuries? How can you be sure you won't drown or that a shark won't approach you?

Sometimes, it seems more logical to swim away. To save those big waves for the risk-takers, the adventurers, and instead stick with paddling around in those smaller waves, the ones that don't carry much potential for danger. That's where most people swim, anyway, and you wouldn't want to risk looking like the "crazy one," would you?

When I was a teen who had a heart filled with dreams, there were times when I felt like the crazy one. The writing career looked like that massive wave. It didn't make sense financially. But I knew, if I neglected to go all in and take the plunge, then I'd miss out on the incredible potential for impact. I'd always wonder what would've happened—if only I hadn't allowed fear and unbelief to hold me back.

In Ben Carson's book *Think Big: Unleashing Your Potential for Excellence*, he says, "It does not matter where we come from or what we look like. If we recognize our abilities, are willing to learn and to use what we know in helping others, we will always have a place in the world."[23]

You see, our place in the world—our life's purpose—is connected to the way God has designed us to impact this world for His glory. Living in His will has never been safe, comfortable, or easy. Living for His purpose requires more effort than if we were to choose waves that can help us float through life instead.

But we were never created to float. We were equipped with the strength—and with the faith—to rise, to face the challenge, and to embrace the impact zone.

And it's here we discover our greatest opportunity for impact.

Hitting Fast Forward

At the beginning of this chapter, I said how I wished I could give my childhood self a sneak peek into my future. Let's pretend, for a moment, it's possible. That God has given us a fast forward button. We can use this button to have a small preview of what our lives will look like at any age.

I know, I know, it's silly. Just bear with me, okay?

So let's say you have this button in your hand. Maybe it looks like an old tape recorder or something similar. (Google it if you don't know what that looks like. Sometimes I forget how old I've become.) As soon as you hit that fast forward button, *whoosh!* Adrenaline pumps through your veins as you're whirled into a new time and place at the speed of light. Your hair flies everywhere from the sudden motion. But that doesn't matter because no one sees you. Just like Ebenezer Scrooge in *A Christmas Carol*, you are merely an onlooker of the scene before you, and you watch as your future self carries on in a typical day of her life at work.

What do you see? Is your future self happy at work? Passionate about her job? Does this job grant her the opportunity to use her skills, her strengths, to make a difference, and in what ways?

Maybe you tried hitting that fast forward button, but for some reason, a scene never appeared. You weren't whisked away. You're still sitting on the couch or sipping a coffee at

Starbucks or lounged by the beach (I'll try not to be jealous of you). You can't seem to picture what your future job looks like because you have no idea what God is calling you to do.

And that's okay.

You can start where you are with what you have. Confide in your parents, mentors, or counselors and ask them to point you in the right direction. Maybe they see skills that you're blind to. Finding your greatest potential for impact might be a process. And it's a process to undergo while seeking God first, giving Him permission to navigate your journey.

It doesn't need to be complicated. We can shine God's light in any profession. And some people may be called to use their impact zone as a side gig instead of their main career. For example, if you have an outgoing personality and are a people-person, you could volunteer at a nursing home. If you're into baking, you could bake cookies and sell them to raise money for a family in need. The possibilities are endless.

In Ben Caron's book, *Gifted Hands,* he wrote, "God created us, loves us and wants to help us to realize our potential so that we can be useful to others."[24]

You can discover your potential by asking this question: *How can I use my skills to add value to others?*

If God is calling you to take a risk on the impact zone, then embrace it with all you've got. He's equipped you with the muscles you need to thrive, not just float.

Then, in your future, perhaps you will come across a notebook from your childhood as well—the page where you described your dreams—and you'll see it. A glimpse of who you were meant to become had already birthed inside of you, even as a child.

Perhaps that's because our Creator already had in mind how He gifted us to influence others in our impact zones.

Chapter Eight
Do Dreams Originate from God?

Several years ago, there was a fifteen-year-old girl who had no choice but to stay home and lead an immobile life. She could hardly even leave her bed because of a condition called cytomegalovirus, which is a crazy word that basically means she couldn't do anything or go anywhere. She had to remain homebound so that she wouldn't expose herself to germs and compromise her weak immune system. All she could do was sleep.

That's what her life looked like for two years. And there didn't seem to be much hope this would ever change.[25]

Can you imagine how difficult that would be? I mean, having to stay in lockdown during COVID was hard enough! But to have a condition as a teen that blew away the flames of any dreams in her heart, except this girl didn't allow her condition to blow them out. In fact, it was during this period that a new dream ignited within her.

A dream to become a singer. To spread hope and God's love through the power of music. She chose to see her future self doing just that—singing before thousands of people. Writing and recording her own songs, no longer held captive from this paralyzing condition.[26]

Now, if a typical realist heard her talk about this dream, they probably would've tried to wake this girl up to reality. "You're too weak to sing," they could have said. Maybe that person would've shook her head and offered this girl a pitiful, bless-your-heart kind of pout. "Sweetie, your immune system is severely compromised. There's no way you can risk singing before thousands of people. Not to mention, as a Christian, the aspiration of becoming a singer is self-centered. That won't help you live the humble life Jesus has commanded us to live."

As far as I know, this girl didn't have a realist who tried to blow out the flames of her dreams. But there were times when she was tempted to do just that. She could hardly walk up the stairs without becoming short of breath. It was often difficult for her to imagine an improvement in her health, that her life would ever return to normal again.

She even felt like her dreams were a joke.[27]

But this teenager continued to seek God first. As she did, the fire of faith enlarged those dreams, feeding those embers. This faith enabled her to trust that God had placed those dreams on her heart for a reason.

And I'm sure glad she kept that fire ablaze. If she hadn't, then the Christian music industry wouldn't have had the honor of introducing Lauren Daigle's inspirational and worship music to the world. Millions of people—both believers and nonbelievers alike—would have never received the message of hope through her songs.[28]

A *selfish* dream? I don't think so. A dream placed on her heart to spur her in the right direction? Absolutely.

But it's not wrong of us, as Christians, to ask if a certain dream was placed on our heart by God or if it is merely an extension of our flesh. So how can we know the difference?

A Greater Purpose

If your great-grandparents are still alive and they told you they plan to have more kids, what would your response be? After recovering from your burst of laughter, only to realize they weren't joking, you'd probably give some remark like, "No disrespect, but I'm starting to think your old age is having a negative effect on your mind." Okay, so maybe you wouldn't say that to your great-grandparents. But you would at least *think* that, right?

Yet as crazy as it sounds, this was the dream Abram and Sarah had when they were approaching one-hundred years old. (You can read their story in Genesis 15–18). Surprisingly, this *wasn't* a result of their aging minds. It was a dream given by God Himself. They weren't called to have another child just so they could be blessed, but through this child, millions more would be blessed for generations to come.

Because it was through this child's family line that Jesus would someday arrive.

That was the greater purpose of their dream. A purpose we are still being blessed by and benefiting from today.

Who else had a purpose-filled dream?

How about Martin Luther King Jr.? His dream didn't stem from selfish motives. He didn't step up to that podium before hundreds of thousands of people and declare, "I have a dream . . ." so his story could be read in history books. It wasn't a fantasy of his to be known as the man who delivered that iconic motivational speech during the Civil Rights Movement.

Martin Luther King Jr.'s dream—to live in a world free from racial discrimination—led to equality among African Americans and brought about much-needed changes within America.[29]

That was the greater purpose of his passion.

Now, I can't proclaim that *every* dream is connected to a greater purpose, especially those we held as children. Can you recall any of those out-of-the-box aspirations you once had? I can recall one of mine.

One day, when I was in Sunday school, my teacher asked the class what we wanted to be when we grew up, and then she passed around coloring pages that reflected those aspirations. Can you guess what the picture was on my coloring page?

No, it wasn't a picture of an author or an actress. It was a picture of an angel. (Although I really wanted to be both a dog *and* an angel. But maybe the teacher didn't have a picture of a dog.)

Now, don't make fun of me. I was probably three at the time. And I'd like to believe that I have grown up to become a very fine angel, *thankyouverymuch*.

Obviously, some of our childhood dreams are an extension of our greater-than-life imagination and childlike ignorance. There might even be embers of dreams that never fizzle with age, and yet they aren't necessarily the ones God has called us to pursue. And since Jeremiah 17:9 tells us *"the human heart is the most deceitful of all things,"* how is it to be trusted to lead us in the right direction?

To state it bluntly, it's not.

Following our dreams should never come before *following our God.* Rather, as we follow God and seek Him first, He can then reveal to us the dreams He wants us to pursue.

Yes, our hearts are an extension of our sinful nature, but isn't God the One who created our hearts to begin with? And when we accepted Jesus Christ as our Savior, our hearts were washed by the blood of the Lamb. We have been given a new heart to replace our former selfish one (Ezekiel 36:26).

So, yes, I do believe God can place certain dreams on our hearts. Ones that are connected to a greater purpose than to feed our selfish motives.

But to pursue the right ones, we must first understand how to listen to the right nudges.

Listening to the Right Nudges

What is a dream, anyway?

No, I'm not talking about the ones you have while sleeping, the dreams of conquering dragons and owning a castle. (Although how cool would it be if those dreams actually came true!) I'm referring to the ones that ignite a passion within. The fantasies that are an extension of our deepest longings, giving us a glimpse of what *could be.* These dreams first sprout in our hearts, become conjured in our imaginations, and then motivate our actions.

There's nothing wrong with having dreams; in fact, it's all a part of how God has created us in His image. Didn't God use His imagination to shape this entire world into being? Genesis 1:2 tells us, before Creation took place, *"The earth was formless and empty, and darkness covered the deep waters."*

But the Creator had a dream—to bask this darkness in light. He must have first imagined what this would look like before He acted, don't you think? He could've imagined the majestic glistening oceans, the array of colors broadcasted in the Garden, the birds that would fly against the canvas of a blue sky while singing His praises.

The act of creation was part of God's plan.

I believe, when we are called to bring God's plan into fulfillment, He works with us in the same way. He plants a dream inside of us. A desire. Then we can use our imaginations to envision what this dream could look like if it is acted upon.

But here's the thing—and this is why a lot of Christians don't believe in the idea of pursuing their dreams. Just like with any good thing in life, the Enemy has twisted and perverted what God originally intended to be used for good. He's caused people to use their imaginations to further the Enemy's "kingdom" rather than God's. To commit crimes and sins instead of pursuing works that could lead people to Christ.

Yes, our hearts *can* have desires that fall in line with God's Word and His will—or we can have desires that give way to an empty life of self-profit and self-destruction.

So how can we listen to the right nudges—and what does this even mean?

We can start by applying the truth found in Galatians 5:16–17:

> *So I say, let the Holy Spirit guide your lives. Then you won't be doing what your sinful nature craves. The sinful nature wants to do evil, which is just the opposite of what the Spirit wants. And the Spirit gives us desires that are the opposite of what the sinful nature desires. These two forces are constantly fighting each other, so you are not free to carry out your good intentions.*

The Enemy can give us longings that result in idolatry. Selfish ambition. Envy. Wild parties among others. (You can find the full list in Galatians 5:19–21.)

But then the Holy Spirit plants longings within us that result in *"love, joy, peace, patience, kindness, goodness, faithfulness, gentleness, and self-control"* (Galatians 5:22–24).

So when we have a dream, let's ask ourselves—if this is acted upon, what would the fruit of it be? Self-praise? Or would it contribute to *God's* praise?

Children of God whose hearts have been cleansed by Jesus' blood have *"nailed the passions and desires of their sinful nature to his cross and crucified them there"* (Galatians 5:24). This means we are free to *"follow the Spirit's leading in every part of our lives"* (v. 25).

In other words, we are free to listen to the *right* nudges. Those dreams that can spur us on to fulfill our role as influencer.

Your "Success" Story

I didn't include Lauren Daigle's story in this chapter to glorify her and her success, but rather to inspire you to live your *own* success story. But I'm not referring to "success" in terms of how the world views success: Achievements. Approval of others. Worldly gain, wealth, and prosperity. *Success,* in the kingdom, looks far different.

Worldly success asks, "How many trophies do you have to your name?" Kingdom success asks instead, "How many souls have you won for the kingdom?"

Worldly success may advise, "Live the kind of life that deserves a page on Wikipedia." Kingdom success advises instead, "Live the kind of life that can influence people for eternity and perhaps for generations to come."

Worldly success asks, "Are you building your platform?" Kingdom success asks instead, "Are you building disciples?"

Which kind of success are your dreams driving you to grasp?

Now, I'm not trying to imply that material success is evil, sinful, and should have no place in the life of a Christian. If it comes with the territory of aiming for eternal success, then there's nothing wrong with that. Perhaps that's just another way God will bless you in this life.

But as you begin to evaluate the dreams on your heart, I hope you will reflect on your motivations for pursuing them. One way you can do this is by doing the exercise *"I want to...So that I can . . ."*

I want to...*start an orphanage in the Philippines.*

So that I can...*provide a home for children whose parents are unable to tend to their needs.*

Don't be afraid to dream. Don't be afraid to trust that the same God who conjured this entire planet, this entire universe, into creation can breathe life into your Spirit-led longings and visions as well. You serve a God *"who is able, through his mighty power at work within us, to accomplish infinitely more than we might ask or think"* (Ephesians 3:20).

I can't wait to hear about your success story some day! And who knows? I might even share it to inspire readers in future books of mine.

Chapter Nine
Your Place on the Team

I wasn't the type of girl in gym class to be picked first for a team. That didn't offend me though. There are some flaws about ourselves we learn to accept over time, and one of mine is sports are just not my thing.

I did, however, compete on a competitive cheer squad when I was in school—and although I was frequently tempted to skip practice, my parents never let me. They knew if I was gone the routine would falter. My stunt group would be unable to perform their stunts.

My role on the squad was important.

The same principle applied when I was involved in theater. When an actor had to miss rehearsal, there would be an awkwardness to the scenes. Their lack of presence could throw off the dance choreography. The actors scripted to interact with the one missing found it challenging to react without the prompts presented in the unspoken lines.

Do you see how necessary it is for each team player to fulfill his or her position? Without a cheerleader's role as the base in a stunt, that group can't throw the flier into the air. Even in theater, where there are multiple ensemble actors, each one is chosen for a reason and is given instructions for the scene. The ensemble actors must work together in rhythm and unity for the scene to be a success.

In the same way, everyone who is in Christ Jesus is connected to one another and has been assigned an important role to fulfill.

1 Corinthians 12:27 tells us *"all of you together are Christ's body, and each of you is a part of it."* What does this part look like? It varies for each person based on their gifts and skills, but it involves serving and contributing to the health of the Body in some way. Our team goal isn't to perform or compete, but to use the Body's hands and feet to reach the lost, extending the gospel throughout the ends of the earth. But we can't function properly if someone fails to fulfill his or her role. You see, we each have a responsibility on this team, and we must learn to work together in this like-minded mission if we hope to grow strong, healthy, and perform our duties.

As a young woman, how can you discover what your place on this " team" might look like?

The Winning Philosophy

I've never been the competitive type of person. You know those types—the ones who are driven to win every game they play, even if they're only playing for fun. But if you're that kind of person, you may be curious to hear Tony Dungy's secret on how to win. Listen closely because this former NFL coach has had his fair share of winning games. He's earned his teams a total of 148 wins throughout the years, including a win at the Super Bowl.[30]

Not too shabby, right?

Tony Dungy first played for the Pittsburgh Steelers in his early twenties before he went on to become the head coach for the Indianapolis Colts.[31] It was during this time of coaching that he adapted his winning philosophy. His secret to attaining multiple victories.

Dungy wanted to create an encouraging atmosphere among his players—a place where they could each strive to perform their best as they worked together as a team. *Team unity* will always triumph over talent, according to him.[32]

But doesn't every good head coach drill the principle of teamwork into their players?

Possibly, but Dungy specifically understood this idea involved more than having his players work together. Rather, he needed to emphasize the key to unlocking their true potential.

And that key was *selflessness*.

I love the way he describes teamwork:

Teamwork doesn't mean you don't have individual goals. It means you're willing to put your individual goals behind the goals of the team. If you can do that, you'll be a great teammate, and you'll have great teamwork. That's what we're always looking for on our football team—people who can put their individual goals and hopes behind those of the team, which are winning and being the best team that we can be.[33]

There are some athletes who only play to show off their own skills. Some athletes play to achieve their personal goals of success in the arena of sports. But Dungy knew the it's-all-about-me attitude would only serve as a stumbling block for the teams he coached. It would prevent them from truly refining their abilities.

In a podcast interview with Positive University, Dungy said, "When you're playing for each other versus yourself, you're more likely to win."[34]

What does it mean to play for each other versus yourself? It means the athletes's individual goals are created to support the mission of the team as a whole: To win the next game. Not to build their name as an individual, but to build the name of their team. Even if that includes stepping out of the way so a teammate's strength can outperform their own. Even if that looks like sacrificing their own craving for praise and instead stepping aside so their teammate can take the final shot.

Selflessness.

Since Tony Dungy's winning philosophy has proven so successful, I couldn't help but wonder—what would it look like if every member of the Body of Christ applied the same principle? Not in sports, but in life in general. Pursuing our individual callings for the purpose of strengthening the family of Christ and to support our mission. What if we strove to use our strengths, skills, and gifts to build God's name rather than our own?

Tony Dungy isn't just known for being one of the winningest coaches in NFL history. He is also known for putting faith and family first throughout his twenty-eight-year career in the NFL. The principles he's learned about teamwork during this time have motivated him in his faith walk as well.[35]

"It's human nature to put yourself first," he said. "But Romans tells us not to think like the world thinks but to transform your thinking. That's really what you have to constantly try to do."[36]

Your Spot Is Needed

I'm sure you've heard that famous saying "There is no *I* in team!" Coaches drill this saying into their players' minds to remind them to work together as a whole. To have team unity. Why must athletes constantly be reminded of this principle?

If I had to guess, I'd assume it's because of our natural tendency to focus on *self* first. Just like Dungy said—the idea of working together as a team goes against our human nature. And it doesn't help that we live in a culture very much about *I* right now!

"How can *I* have a bigger social media presence?"

"How can *I* achieve my dreams and grow my bank account?"

Now, I'm not saying it's wrong to consider our own wants and needs. We do need to make a living, after all. However, we must never allow these self-motivated goals to prevent us from playing our part in the kingdom of God. This spot has been saved for us—purchased by the blood of Christ—so why should we want to ignore it and never use our potential to the fullest?

Obviously, I've been speaking in analogy language throughout this chapter. We aren't *really* playing an actual sport. (Thank God! I'd hate for my lack of athletic skills to hold us back.) So what does it look like to win in God's kingdom? We can't play successfully unless we first know what it is we're playing *for*.

Are we playing to win a trophy? To gain a certain amount of material wealth? Not quite. In fact, kingdom success doesn't use the same measurements as worldly success.

I love the way Tony Dungy puts it in his memoir, *Quiet Strength:*

God gives each of us unique gifts, abilities, and passions. How well we use those qualities to have an impact on the world around us determines how 'successful' we really are. If we get caught up in chasing what the world defines as success, we can use our time and talent to do some great things. We might even become famous. But in the end, what will it mean?

God's definition of success is really one of significance—the significant difference our lives can make in the lives of others. The significance doesn't show up in won-loss records, long resumes, or the trophies gathering dust on our mantels. It's found in the hearts and lives of those we've come across who are in some way better because of the way we lived.[37]

The reason why our selfish goals can distract us from winning in God's kingdom is because they are a conflict to our calling as a Christian. They keep us from supporting our mission as a team:

To live our lives for the good of others.

To make a difference.

To shine God's light into this dark world, impacting lives for eternity, and continuing Jesus' ministry.

God has chosen you and me to play a role on His team in this time of history. This is where our purpose is found. It's why we were created and gifted with a unique set of skills and strengths. So we can all work together to accomplish this like-minded mission.

Feelings of insignificance, and even comparison, have no place in the kingdom of God because they're lies. Your spot is needed. Your place on the team matters, and no one else can fill it the way you can.

We are reminded of the significance of our unique role in 1 Corinthians 12:15–20:

> *If the foot says, "I am not a part of the body because I am not a hand," that does not make it any less a part of the body. And if the ear says, "I am not part of the body because I am not an eye," would that make it any less a part of the body? If the whole body were an eye, how would you hear? Or if your whole body were an ear, how would you smell anything? But our bodies have many parts, and God has put each part just where he wants it. How strange a body would be if it had only one part! Yes, there are many parts, but only one body.*

No Time to Waste

In the small town where I grew up, Friday night high school football or basketball games were the preferred hangout. Especially for teens. But when I was a kid, there was one word I used to describe these games: *Miserable.* I often had no choice but to accompany my parents as they went to support my older sisters's cheerleading for their teams. We must have stepped into another dimension in these games or something, because seriously, it was like time never passed in those bleachers. The seconds…went on…*forever.*

Sometimes, it feels like life is going to continue *forever* as well. Like it's merely a never-ending game composed of endless quarters.

But the truth is, we don't know how long this life is going to last. We could already be in the third quarter. Or we could still be in the first quarter. It's not our job to know *exactly* when Jesus will return, but we do know this:

When He returns, it will be *"like a thief in the night"* (1 Thessalonians 5:2, ESV). Unexpected. Sudden. Inescapable. When that buzzer sounds—or, rather, when the *trumpet* sounds—there's not going to be any time left on the scoreboard. No chance for overtime to grant additional seconds.

1 Thessalonians 5:6 (ESV) warns us to *"keep awake and be sober."* So why are so many Christians still sitting on the sidelines? There are souls to reach. There is work to do in God's kingdom. Matthew 24:14 tells us Jesus won't return until the gospel is carried throughout the entire world.

And who is going to carry the message other than the Body of Christ?

As a teen, you don't need to wait a few years before you jump in the game and fulfill your influencer duties. I challenge you to *discover* your gifts: What is your sweet spot? Is there a subject in school you've always been fascinated with? What areas do you tend to excel in?

And then you can *develop* these gifts: Are there courses you can take to help you improve this skill? Internships or job shadows you can apply for? Do you know anyone in this field who can serve as a mentor for you?

Tony Dungy was right when he said, "Success to me is doing everything you can do with the skills and the gifts God gives you."[38]

As your team player, I want to encourage you to give it your all. You've got this. We're in this together. Striving forward in our like-minded mission to spread the gospel. And guess what the good news is? We've already had a sneak peek at the results of this game. According to the Bible, we're on the winning team. Our enemy doesn't stand a chance against us—*especially* when we are united as one.

But to effectively defeat the darkness, we must all work together, using our unique gifts to spread God's light. There is no room for *I*. Let's play as though the buzzer could sound at any moment…because it could.

There's no time to waste.

Our team is counting on us.

Review

- Let's thrive in the impact zone—the place where we excel in our strengths, move toward our God-given dreams, and use our gifts to influence this world for Christ.

- Our God-given dreams are connected to our calling. These dreams can steer us in the right direction and give us an opportunity to carry out our influencer duties.

- Each of us have been assigned a unique position in the Body of Christ, and it's our responsibility to discover how our gifts can support our like-minded mission to further the gospel.

Replenish

"God has given each of you a gift from his great variety of spiritual gifts. Use them well to serve one another" (1 Peter 4:10).

"Don't compare yourself with others. Just look at your own work to see if you have done anything to be proud of. You must each accept the responsibilities that are yours" (Galatians 6:4–5, ERV).

"However, he has given each one of us a special gift through the generosity of Christ" (Ephesians 4:7).

"For we are God's handiwork, created in Christ Jesus to do good works, which God prepared in advance for us to do" (Ephesians 2:10, NIV).

"The human body has many parts, but the many parts make up one whole body. So it is with the body of Christ" (1 Corinthians 12:12).

Respond
Influencer Challenge

Use your sphere of influence on social media by sparking a discussion about this chapter with your friends! I challenge you to write a post that answers the following question. Be sure to use the hashtag #BecomeAnInfluencer in your response!

If you aren't on social media, no worries! You can participate in the same challenge among your friends in real life.

How can we further God's kingdom by following our God-given dreams and developing our gifts? What might this look like?

Part Four
Making the Most of Your Youth

Chapter Ten
Setting the Right Foundation

"**D**o you know what your name means?"

A stranger approached me with this question when I was fifteen years old and visiting a friend's church. We were gathered with the congregation at the altar during praise and worship. I had never seen this twenty-some-thing-year-old before. The question wasn't one I received every day from a stranger, so as you can imagine, I was a little taken aback.

After telling this young woman that I didn't know the meaning of my name, she replied, "God told me to tell you that He hand-selected your name for a reason." And then she encouraged me to research the meaning of my name at home. (That was before I had an iPhone; otherwise, my eagerness would've compelled me to look it up right then and there!)

Fast forward thirteen years. Just two days ago, I was at

the altar during praise and worship at my church. Another stranger prayed for me, and afterward this lady told me that my name was significant.

Coincidence?

I don't think so.

What's even more crazy is the revelation I had while looking up my name's meaning after that first encounter. I learned that my name, Tessa, means "one who harvests."[39] This was mind-blowing. I was reminded of my favorite Bible verse, Ecclesiastes 3:1: *"For everything there is a season, a time for every activity under heaven."* That Scripture has provided encouragement and hope for me since I first discovered it in sixth grade. At the time, I needed the reminder that every season in my life was serving to fulfill a purpose only God could see from His vantage point.

Now, I may not know much about farming, but I do know that timing is vital to producing a good harvest. It's the farmer's responsibility to know which steps and tasks to perform during each season. The first step in this process involves preparing the ground. Setting the right foundation. Because without this foundation in place then the ground would never be ready to produce the right crops.

After I discovered my name meant *harvester,* I became intentional about spending my teen years wisely. You see, I was now inspired to take steps toward preparing the ground. I wanted to become who God created me to be, to prepare for the calling He placed on my life.

Time was of the essence.

The teen years provide the perfect opportunity to build this foundation and prepare for the future. And although your name might not mean *harvester,* I still believe God wants you to prepare for your future harvest as well. So how can you make the most of your youth by setting the right foundation for your future?

Training to Be King

When you think about the character David from the Bible, how do you typically picture him? Perhaps you envision a mighty warrior. Respected king. Courageous giant-slayer. A man after God's own heart. Although David can be described as all these things, we must remember that he was not born into a royal position.

Before this noble king could step into the luxuries of a palace, he first lived the smelly life of a shepherd. Before this courageous warrior could conquer a giant, he first needed to gain victory against a few lions and bears.

The character traits and qualities David needed in his role as ruler were developed during his youth while out in the fields tending his father's sheep. It's in the solitude of these fields where he built the foundation of his faith and relationship with God. Because who else was there, other than the sheep, for him to talk with? It was during those moments of playing the harp for the sheep that he learned things that would further his future service as the future King of Israel.

God knew, all along, the destiny he had in mind for young David. But for David to be equipped to carry out his leadership, his faith needed to be strengthened. A character of responsibility, patience, and humility needed to be built. These muscles needed to develop because they would come in handy during his future.

The most important of all, of course, was the foundation David built in his relationship with God. In fact, I don't believe he would've been anointed king if he had not used his youth wisely in this manner. What if he hadn't learned how to relate to God as his own Shepherd while working in those lonely fields? Or what if he had never relied on His strength to help him defeat those wild animals? The harvest God had in store for David's life may have never received the right nourishment. The foundation for his future would've never securely formed.

But as David went on, day-by-day, carrying out his shepherd tasks and responsibilities—as boring as they may have been—he was proving himself to be faithful in this small role. Meanwhile, God saw the bigger picture. God knew He was training David for a role that would carry a far larger impact. He was testing to see if David would have what it took to become the anointed King of Israel.

And it was because of David's faithfulness to pursue the right foundation during his youth that God did, in fact, move him into the honorable calling of king.

Common Trait of a Farmer

After learning more about farming as I researched this chapter, I've reached a conclusion:

I was not called to be a farmer.

Shocking, right?

Not only are farmers required to work in the hot sun day-in and day-out, use heavy machinery (I've never even mowed the lawn), and are likely, as my dad says, "sweating bullets" the whole time, but they can never make excuses. They can't wake up one morning and decide the day's work can wait until tomorrow.

Time is of the essence. Farmers know, if they hope to see a harvest, they must get out there and plant the seeds. And if they hope to plant the seeds, then they must first prepare the ground by plowing the dirt and cultivating the land.

What is the common trait these farmers possess?

Patience. Perseverance. (Yes, I do realize that is two traits, not one.) The reason they arise at the crack of dawn to labor out in their fields is not usually to fulfill some childhood dream of theirs, although maybe that's part of it, but because they can see the long-term pay off. They must trust today's groundbreaking work (gosh, terrible pun) will lead to next fall's harvest.

For the rest of us who have not been called to be farmers, it can be quite a challenge to carry out these disciplines. Where can we find the motivation to prepare for our futures, especially when we don't even know what our "harvest" may look like?

Think back to David's story. He didn't know God was conditioning him to be king, and yet he still chose to remain faithful, disciplined, and diligent in his daily responsibilities and walk with God.

Another example from the Old Testament is Joseph. When he was a teen, he was given a glimpse, in his dreams, of what the "harvest" would look like in his life. He knew even his brothers would someday bow to him. Imagine that! But before Joseph could be ready to become launched into this high position as leader in Egypt, he first needed to learn Humility and Service 101 in his unexpected roles as both a slave and a prisoner.

It's a no-brainer that neither David nor Joseph grew up in today's *I-want-it-now* society. Because those traits are especially hard to acquire for those of us who have, in fact, been raised in this microwave culture and expect quick results. No longer do we need to kill our own chickens and toil in the kitchen for hours to prepare a meal for our family; we can simply hop over to the closest Chick-Fil-A. Or, better yet, whip out our phones and place an order for those chicken fingers to be delivered to our doorsteps.

Done and done.

To put it bluntly: We're accustomed to getting what we want at the push of a button. It's like—we want to defeat the giant, we just don't want the practice giants that come before it. We want to be ruler of Egypt, we just don't want those years of being a slave and a prisoner.

But when God places a calling on our lives, it doesn't necessarily arrive assembled all in one day. It's not delivered to our front porches wrapped in shiny packaging, a pretty bow, and a tag that says, "Open Immediately!"

Rather, *the journey of discovering our calling is a process.* It's during this process—of allowing God to transform us—we become the right person to carry out our unique role as influencer. And during this process we gain that farmer-like ability to see through a long-term perspective, trusting our hard work will pay off.

But only when the time is right.

This Season Matters

I get it. You have a heart full of dreams. You long to be used by God in a mighty way. It may be painful to hear that the harvest could take time. The good news, however, is this:

The journey to receiving your harvest begins now.

Sure, the current season of your life may appear mundane. But what if, through those weekly soccer practices, God is training you in diligence and perseverance? Or what if, as you help your younger siblings with their homework, God is instilling within you the patience of a teacher?

I know it's difficult to set this foundation, but it's during our youth when God can especially help us become all He has called us to be. We can't expect to be brought into our life's assignments until the proper training has taken place.

So if you've been itching to rush ahead and collect your harvest, I encourage you to heed the advice found in the following verses:

"So let's not get tired of doing what is good. At just the right time we will reap a harvest of blessing if we don't give up" (Galatians 6:9).

"Be patient, therefore, brothers, until the coming of the Lord. See how the farmer waits for the precious fruit of the earth,

being patient about it, until it receives the early and the late rains. You also, be patient. Establish your hearts, for the coming of the Lord is at hand" (James 5:7–8, ESV).

This current season of your life matters. I challenge you to make the most of your youth by setting the right foundation. Remain faithful where God has you by drawing close to Him and studying His Word. Allow Him to work on your heart, develop the character within you, and guide you as you learn necessary, practical skills.

If you do this, I believe you will see a payoff for your diligence and faithfulness just like David did. And only then will you be prepared to collect the growth, the harvest, that is sure to arrive in God's perfect season.

Chapter Eleven
What Seeds Are You Planting?

N early every morning over the past six weeks—after hitting the snooze button on my alarm a couple times—I've rolled out of bed to tend to my gardening duties. These plants I've watered and nurtured aren't going to be fully developed for a couple more months, but I can't risk even a single day of neglect.

Otherwise, their growth may become stunted.

Okay, so I'm not *actually* referring to an *actual* garden. (Admittedly, I haven't cared for plants since I was a kid, and I had to water my mom's garden as a daily chore!) I'm referring to the writing process of this book. Because this book didn't write itself—although that certainly would've saved me a lot of time. It first began as a seed of an idea two years ago when I was on a personal writing retreat. I knew, from the beginning, I wanted this book to be a non-fiction Christian Living book for teen girls with a motivational slant.

That's the "crop" I'd been hoping to produce.

With that in mind, I took necessary steps toward planting the right seed. The deadline of this book wasn't due for three more months, but if I waited until the week before it was due to begin watering and caring for this seed, there'd be no way it'd bloom in time. (Not to mention, I would be crazy stressed!)

But I'll admit—there have been times when I've woken up and haven't felt like sitting at my desk. Times when I've wanted to curl up and go back to sleep. And times when I've been tempted to neglect the daily watering of *this* seed and work on my fiction project instead. But that novel isn't the one I needed to grow right now, and if I nurtured the wrong seed, then, well, I wouldn't reap the right kind of harvest at the right time.

Okay, enough speaking in analogy language (for now, at least).

The thing is, farmers and gardeners understand this principle. They understand if they hope to reap a certain crop, then they must plant the right seeds. And if they hope those plants will grow into full bloom, then they can't risk even a single day of neglect.

The same principle applies to real life as well. The seeds we plant today should be determined by the harvest we hope to yield tomorrow.

But it's not always easy to keep this up in the real world. Sometimes it's more tempting to roll over in bed, am I right? As comfy as that sounds, laziness isn't the type of harvest neither of us hope to produce with our lives.

So how can we begin our days with intention, and what

kind of seeds can we plant that will grow into the beautiful garden we envision for our futures?

Striving Toward Author Land

I embarked on an adventure I didn't expect in high school.

No, it wasn't an actual physical adventure like a hike or anything. It was a figurative one that led me to where I am today, over a decade later, writing this book.

With my parents's permission, I enrolled in a virtual school in the ninth grade so I could have the time and flexibility to pursue my writing career.

It was exciting at first. Exhilarating to embrace this new adventure of chasing my dreams. I felt like my entire life had led to that moment, and I was ready, full of passionate energy for the journey ahead.

The creative writing course I took through this new school taught techniques that sharpened my craft, and the more I learned, the more I *wanted* to learn. My amazingly supportive parents also enrolled me in an additional writing program, and during this time I launched a blog and set out to write my first full-length novel, *Purple Moon.*

Time ticked by on this new adventure. Along the path, I noticed that the scenery never changed—figuratively speaking. Sure, it was beautiful to admire the rolling hills and lush meadows and flocks of birds surrounding my path, but was this continuous trail leading to anything? Or was I only fooling myself by thinking I could someday become an author? Those warm, fuzzy feelings I once had while first embracing this journey had faded. My senses dulled to the beauty surrounding me, and my leg muscles cramped, weary from the nonstop trekking. Sweat dripped along my forehead as I squinted against the sunlight, struggling to find a potential destination up ahead.

But there was nothing.

I wanted to arrive. Wherever that may have been and whatever that destination looked like. I wanted to be there already.

I turned around and looked behind me. *Should I head back?* I wondered. *Should I return to school with my friends?* There was no guarantee I'd ever arrive in Author Land, anyway, and doubts crowded my mind. "You never should've left your friends to pursue a silly dream," those doubts said. "That wasn't God nudging you. Who do you think you are, thinking you could become a professional writer at your young age? Look around you. You're alone on this journey."

Taking a break from the journey, I presented these doubts to God during my quiet time. I shared my heart with Him. And then I opened my Bible to a random page and read a verse that had never stood out to me before. It was one I discovered in my copy of The Message Bible from Ecclesiastes 11:9 (MSG):

You who are young, make the most of your youth.
Relish your youthful vigor.
Follow the impulses of your heart.
If something looks good to you, pursue it.
But know also that not just anything goes;
You have to answer to God for every last bit of it.

The phrases that jumped out at me? *Make the most of your youth.* Sure, I could've had fun with my friends at school, but would I have been making the *most* of my youth?

Pursue it. I liked that verb. *Pursue.* That implies forward action, momentum, and intentional effort devoted toward reaching a destination. Sounds like the opposite of remaining stagnant, don't you think?

And then the final sentence: *You have to answer to God for every last bit of it.* I wasn't just pursuing Author Land because it sounded fun. It was an adventure I'd embarked on with God's guidance. This part of the verse reminded me why I needed to keep my heart in the right place; I needed to continue putting Him first and allowing Him, rather than my own fleshly desires, to guide my steps.

Now that God had put my doubts to rest, renewed energy flowed through my veins. It was time to embrace the next leg of the journey.

So that's exactly what I did—I returned to the path and kept at it, one step after another, day by day. Years passed until finally the scenery changed.

Author Land glimmered in the distance.

I had finally "arrived."

No, the journey wasn't easy, and it certainly wasn't quick—but that was okay. Because I'd learned an important truth along the way:

The path toward pursuing your calling was never meant to be rushed.

Your Future Garden

Remember the fast forward button we pretended to have in chapter seven? We're going to use that for another exercise. I want you to hit that button again and imagine standing before a garden you've planted. (Some of you, like myself, may have to use some strong imagination power if you don't naturally have a green thumb!) You can decide how big your garden is, how it's designed, and the types of plants and flowers it displays. Is it an elaborate garden or more simplistic? Are there non-plant elements, such as benches or stones?

As you breathe in the sweet aroma, relief floods your soul. It's the I-really-just-did-this kind of relief. There's nothing quite like that sense of accomplishment after devoting days into endless hard work.

It's all paid off now. Those hours of toiling in the hot sun led you to this very moment. Now you have the pleasure of basking in the beauty of your garden and enjoying the fruits of your labor. Perhaps quite literally!

Okay, time to return to the present. You may have already caught on, but your future garden isn't meant to be a literal one. Although I'd certainly be impressed if it is! Rather, it's going to illustrate the one you're going to grow throughout your lifetime.

What kind of garden do you desire to see in your future? What are the varieties of flowers that will bloom, giving off an aroma to be enjoyed and admired by those around you? Will the crops you produce inspire others to plant their own as well?

Gardeners understand they must map out a plan before getting to work. The types of flowers, vegetables, and plants a gardener hopes to grow will determine the type of seeds they plant.

So let's say you hope to someday launch an outreach ministry. Or perhaps you'd like to become a full-time mom or start your own business. Or maybe all three of those sound like good possibilities.

Now, here's a powerful, mind-blowing thought:

You have the power and potential as a teen to plant the seeds that can produce the harvest you hope to enjoy in your future. You can decide today how you hope others will feel when they're around you. Will they sense the fragranced aroma you carry from your relationship with Christ? Will your cheerful personality illuminate God's joy into their own lives?

With those results in mind, you can then decide which steps to take—which seeds to plant and cultivate—that will produce the intended character, career, and ministry.

Does this sound a little "out there" to you? Don't worry, I didn't make this up. This principle is found in Galatians 6:7–8 (ESV): *"Do not be deceived: God is not mocked, for whatever one sows, that will he also reap. For the one who sows to his own flesh will from the flesh reap corruption, but the one who sows to the Spirit will from the Spirit reap eternal life."*

You've already planted some seeds in your life. Did you know that? We plant seeds in our thoughts. Actions. Words. The way we treat people. The choices we make in our free time. The habits we've established. Whether good or evil, life or death, we plant and cultivate seeds throughout every day of our lives.

But many people fail to realize this principle. They're blind to seeing how their decision to scroll through social media all day, every day could reap an undesirable harvest that includes laziness and poverty. We must remain awake and aware of the seeds we plant and cultivate—not only aware, but *intentional.*

We can do this by envisioning our future garden and asking ourselves: Are the decisions I'm making today, this very hour, going to yield the right kind of garden? How will these choices impact not only my future, but my eternity as well? How will they impact my future health and relationships?

Now, here's a word of warning: *A garden is not grown overnight.*

Think back to the story I shared from my own adventure toward Author Land. Each day, I had to choose to take one step after another, even on the days when I couldn't imagine ever arriving at the destination. But every day's hard work brought me that much closer to a healthy garden.

If we develop this bird's eye perspective, then we can imagine our future garden, and we can trust today's choices will bring us closer toward reaping that harvest.

We can't see how seeds work beneath the ground as they spread their roots. That's out of our sight. Regardless, we continue giving it the water and sunlight it needs to flourish because soon, the shoot will sprout through the dirt. And the plant will blossom into the beautiful flower we had in mind all along.

Beginning with the End in Mind

Earlier, I mentioned how I've had to work on this book every day so I can reach my anticipated deadline. Doing this has required me to think in reverse. I considered the book's word count, and then I calculated how many words I'd need to write each week to reach the deadline in time.

I've had to begin with the end in mind.

As a teen, you're at the start of your journey. A meadow extends before you—a blank canvas for your imagination. It's just waiting for you to dig in and get to work planting and cultivating, bringing life to your future garden. How can you plant seeds with the end in mind, and what will this look like, practically speaking?

As you seek God first, asking Him for wisdom and guidance concerning your future, I recommend writing down your God-given dreams. You can then describe the woman you'd like to become, the difference you hope to make with your life, and how you will impact those around you. Don't be afraid to be specific.

From there, work in reverse—just like I had to do with this book. How can you break down that big picture idea into concrete goals and weekly tasks? That will help you determine where to invest your efforts.

It may be helpful to evaluate your life. The choices and habits you're making and how your time is spent. For example, have you formed an unintentional habit of sitting with only your friends at lunch? If so, maybe you can try to plant a seed in someone else's life during this time by moving to a new table and talking with a classmate who looks lonely.

If you've discovered you spend too many hours on TikTok in the evenings, consider planting a new seed instead. For instance, if you're hoping to become a professional basketball player, perhaps you can spend those hours shooting hoops.

I encourage you to especially evaluate the seeds you're planting in your spiritual life—your relationship with Jesus.

And what about your physical health? The words you speak? Your relationships? When you and your siblings grow older, do you hope to have established a good relationship with them?

Are you hoping to be accepted into a good college? Good for you. That, of course, will require intentional effort and hard work by remaining diligent in homework and studying for tests in advance.

These seeds might not look like much within themselves. Some of them are even the size of a grain of salt. But they're powerful. Only, they need to be continuously cared for to flourish the way they were designed to. It all boils down to *diligence* and *perseverance*, even when the results take time to sprout.

I believe your hard work will pay off. Someday, you'll finally have the pleasure to stand before a lush meadow. The garden you've tended to every day of your life.

And it all began with envisioning the end in mind.

Chapter Twelve
Rooted in the Source

I'm the type of person who finds pleasure in checking off tasks on my to-do list. Maybe that's the ambitious side of me. Or maybe that tendency to strive for productivity is a behavior I learned from the mistakes I made when I was younger. Because, really, my natural personality isn't the achiever or go-getter, but when I was a teen, I had to come face-to-face with the consequences that resulted from wasting an entire day watching TV or playing games.

The reality of knowing I could never gain that time back again eventually woke me from my slumber. I wanted to be more intentional with my time management and productivity. Every hour needed to be deposited into that figurative productivity bank account in my head; after all, that was just one way of being the good steward God has called us to be.

But I must admit—over the years, I've taken this tendency to strive hard a little too far. There are days when I want to continue being on the go, checking off those tasks, but my body simply won't let me.

The most recent occurrence of this took place a couple of months ago. I sat on my sofa, head clouded in fog, energy zapped, and a heavy grogginess holding me in place, immobilizing me, making it impossible to make a deposit into my time bank. Since I was first diagnosed with Type 1 diabetes at twenty years old, I've faced many days like this one. Days when my stubborn blood sugars refuse to lower to their normal range. It's because of their stubbornness I develop these flu-like symptoms and am unable to function normally—both physically and mentally.

Not fun.

On this specific day, I could feel the seconds slipping through my fingers. There were deadlines to meet. Emails to respond to. Tasks in my planner waiting for a checkmark. But my body refused, giving me no choice but to feel as though I was being lazy. Unproductive.

This frustrated me. If God wanted me to be productive, why couldn't He allow me to feel better so I could get some work accomplished?

As I vented these frustrations to Him, a revelation occurred to me. It's one I'd already known in my head—especially since it came from one of my favorite passages in the Bible, John 15. But I needed this truth to sink into my spirit. And that truth was this:

God views being productive in a different light than we often do.

You see, our culture has brainwashed us into believing we can only make good use of ourselves when we are constantly on the go. Aiming for new goals. Striving harder. Doing *more*. And while it is biblical to be wise with our days, at the same time, God doesn't measure productivity based on the number of checkmarks by our to-do list.

He uses a different scale altogether.

And what's cool is that this "kingdom productivity," as I like to refer to it, can be achieved even despite our physical limitations. It's only this type of work that'll outlast any success we could ever achieve on our own.

So what does it mean to be productive for His kingdom, and how can you get started?

Rotten Fruit vs. Lasting Fruit

The seconds were slipping away. Like trying to hold a fistful of sand as grains escaped through their fingers, it was impossible to keep a firm grip on that final evening with Jesus. In the Upper Room on the evening before Jesus was crucified, there must have been smiles and laughter, but the bittersweet taste of the impending goodbye probably kept the disciples on the verge of tears. They had less than twenty-four hours to spend with this Man who had transformed their lives.

Jesus Christ, the Messiah. God in flesh.

In the short amount of time they had known Him, Jesus saturated the disciples's lives with meaning. Purpose. They never witnessed such power and love emanate from one person. These disciples had stood on the sidelines, their mouths probably hanging open as they witnessed Jesus setting the captives free, imparting sight to the blind, healing the sick, and casting out demons.

On the eve before Jesus' departure, I wouldn't be surprised if these disciples had swallowed a sip of denial. As Jesus broke the bread during the Last Supper and talked with them about His flesh being given to them, I wonder if Jesus could sense the disciples's refusal to acknowledge this was goodbye. These men didn't exactly ooze with courage, after all.

Jesus must have known, if they were to make it without Him, He'd need to share the secret of how they could remain with Him, even after He was gone. This secret would also unlock their potential to continue furthering His ministry. It'd unlock and unleash an energizing boldness from within, one that had never consumed them before.

This secret was the key to accessing the treasures of love, life, and power that set Jesus apart from other men.

Time was ticking. I can imagine, after they ate the Passover meal, Jesus led this crew out of the Upper Room and into the vineyards outside. An orange strip of sunset could've been painted along the horizon, its fading rays silhouetting Christ as He gave an analogy to these men:

> *"I am the true grapevine, and my Father is the gardener. He cuts off every branch of mine that doesn't produce fruit, and he prunes the branches that do bear fruit so they will produce even more. You have already been pruned and purified by the message I have given you. Remain in me, and I will remain in you. For a branch cannot produce fruit if it is severed from the vine, and you cannot be fruitful unless you remain in me.*

"Yes, I am the vine; you are the branches. Those who remain in me, and I in them, will produce much fruit. For apart from me you can do nothing" (John 15:1–5).

Can you picture this moment? I can see it—the disciples, keeping silent as Jesus once again shares a powerful truth in the guise of an analogy. They couldn't speak because His words needed to sink into their hearts and minds.

There was much truth for them to absorb, and it was a new language for them. Jesus had to use the illustration of a vineyard, something they were familiar with, to help the disciples grasp the concept of abiding in their relationship with Christ. This analogy gave them the "secret" of earning eternal profit rather than merely carnal profit.

These were fishermen and a former tax collector He was speaking with. They had worked hard to earn a living all their lives. And now they were being told any work accomplished apart from Christ basically accounted for nothing. That it's all, figuratively speaking, like rotten fruit.

But the flip side of that? They could still *remain* in Christ. They could live with Him, even when He departed from them in the flesh. If they remained in Christ like a branch rooted in the vine, then the vine would impart into them the life and power they needed to produce abundant and eternal fruit. It's the same life and power Jesus drew from His Father.

The bottom line is we are powerless when we are cut off from Christ, the True Vine. Because it's only by staying grounded in His life and love, attached to our True Source, that we can produce lasting fruit. The only kind of works that'll outlast our lives, bless others, and echo into eternity.

Fake Vine of Self

Now, you may be asking, "But what about people who have earthly success and aren't rooted in Christ?" I don't blame you for wondering this. I mean, there's no denying this world is filled with successful people—many of whom may not know Christ. From appearances, it seems as though these people have everything going for them. How could the works they're producing possibly be deemed as *nothing?*

Let's take another look at the passage above. How did Jesus refer to Himself? As the "true grapevine."That implies there must be "fake vines"we can attach ourselves to as well. So what do these fake vines look like?

If I had one guess, I'd say a fake vine looks like our*selves.* Our flesh. Sinful nature. Ego. Pride. It's this selfish nature that has been an enemy to God's kingdom from the very beginning. It never seeks to profit anything godly; in fact, the result of chasing after its evil desires leads only to death, destruction, and decay.

The fruit from this vine becomes *rotten*. Putrid.

Let me give you one real-life example.

When you think of kings and queens, what comes to mind? Perhaps palaces, castles, crowns, power, and luxury. Sounds like quite the life, don't you think? Kings and queens have been admired and envied for centuries. To live with a royal status—not having to cook your own meals or clean your own bedroom or work for a living, being waited on hand and foot, having your entire wardrobe filled with clothes from the finest designers. I mean, let's be real. Who wouldn't want that kind of lifestyle? That used to sound ideal to me too.

But recently, the admirable reputation attached to the royal status has been tarnished in my mind. And it's all because of a book I've been reading at my grandma's house. My grandma, who is now in her nineties, has always been a history buff, so she was recently given this book as a gift. It's written in textbook-style, describing the history of kings and queens, and it paints quite the historical picture of what life *really* looked like inside of those palaces.[40]

Trust me, it wasn't all rainbows and butterflies. (Or, in this case, tiaras and thrones.) Many of these royals went insane. Some of them, such as King Charles VI of France, believed their bodies were made entirely of glass. There must've been quite an obsession with glass, too, because Princess Alexandra Amelie of Bavaria was convinced she had swallowed an entire glass piano as a child.[41]

I'll do you a favor and spare the gory details of some of the other stories, but let's just say, even though the castles may have sparkled on the outside, they often had the stench of death on the inside.

Quite literally.

Isn't that why Jesus gave us this warning in John 15? When we attach ourselves to the fake vine of self, we shouldn't expect to produce anything other than rotten, smelly fruit. That's because we were never called to root ourselves in our own flesh. That's not where we can receive the nutrients we need to truly thrive and become abundant.

For those of us who have grown up in this "I-can-do-it-all" culture, this truth is a breath of fresh air. We no longer need to strive hard against the current of life, working with all our might to stay afloat. Instead, we can relax. Reach out and grasp the hand of Jesus. The strength He imparts will equip us to rise above the harsh waters of life.

So what does it look like, practically speaking, to remain attached to Christ rather than ourselves? How can we produce this kind of lasting fruit?

We can abide in the True Vine by putting God first in our daily lives. Saturating ourselves with His Word. Staying in communication with Him throughout the day. Keeping our hearts in a state of continual repentance to pure worship of and loving adoration for our Heavenly Father.

Then, the fruit we produce will be a natural byproduct of our unmoving position on the Vine.

What does this fruit look like? Any type of work that can further God's kingdom and lead people to Christ. It may look like being a servant, making disciples, sharing God's love with others, reaching out to the needy, and using our gifts for His glory.

All this fruit—*true* productivity—will outlast our lives, usher in true fulfillment, and bless those around us.

You see, it's not the job of the branch to muster up the courage or energy to produce this type of fruit; its only job is to remain rooted in the Vine.

Later in John 15, Jesus continues His message by discussing how this will help us carry out our life's purpose: *"You didn't choose me. I chose you. I appointed you to go and produce lasting fruit, so that the Father will give you whatever you ask for, using my name. This is my command: Love each other"* (vv. 16–17).

Perhaps that is the reason we have been created...to produce *lasting* fruit. Because it's only in staying attached to

Christ that we overflow with the love we receive from this True Vine. A love that will saturate and ooze out of the fruit we produce. And this love will prompt others to find their position on the True Vine as well.

Pruned by Love

I learned an interesting fact while researching the topic of vineyards.

When vines are cut—or *pruned*—they produce tears known as "weeping vines." Sap drips out of the wounds of the vines in attempt to protect itself from disease.[42]

How cool is that?

What's even more fascinating is seeing how this parallels with John 15. We know, from Jesus' message, that God is our vinedresser, and He tends to us with the same careful attention a husbandman does with its vineyard. In verse two, Jesus said, *"He cuts off every branch of mine that doesn't produce fruit, and he prunes the branches that do bear fruit so they will produce even more."*

But you may be asking: If pruning involves *cutting*—literally causing the vines to weep—then how is that an act of love? What good could come from trimming a healthy vine when the whole goal is to produce fruit?

Great question. I wondered the same. And while searching for answers through handy-dandy Google, I learned another interesting tidbit: Through the act of pruning, the vinedresser cultivates the branches, preparing them to produce *even more* fruit. In fact, if the vinedresser didn't do this, then the branches would become too entangled and ultimately unproductive.[43]

The weeping vines are not evidence of misuse. In fact, it's the opposite because the weeping is evidence there is movement. The sap it produces is healthy and helps to supply nourishment the vine needs to flourish.[44] And even though the vine may appear held back at the moment—even though it seems inactive—it is actually preparing to bear even more fruit.[45]

What if God uses our limitations to prune us as well? Limitations like the chronic illness that sometimes makes me feel less productive.

"Weaknesses" that may make you feel like you can't measure up with the more popular, smarter, outgoing, attractive, or athletic girls in school.

What if the very things we have viewed as hindrances are tools preparing us for growth? What if these setbacks are necessary for equipping us for our life's purpose, to help us become more productive? Perhaps not according to the world's definition of it, but a *fruitful* definition. Because the truth is, being eternally fruitful doesn't often involve reaching the top. It doesn't look like checking off our to-do lists, building our bank accounts, or gaining a verification status on social media.

It involves staying planted in God's Word. Abiding in the True Vine of Christ. Allowing ourselves to become drenched in His love, His life, and His power.

I'll be the first to admit pruning is not a comfortable process. Sometimes it looks like everyone else is striving toward the finish line of success while I'm hobbling through the first meters. But what if God is wanting to remove everything from our lives that could stifle our growth in Him? Can't we trust the vinedresser's intention is to care for the branches, preparing them for their true purpose?

During this time, let's not strive to produce through our own strength; instead, we need to remain still. Sure, we may want to squirm. We may even be tempted to attach ourselves to the fake vine of self, especially as we witness other branches having great success in doing just that. But we need to allow the uncomfortable to draw us even closer to the True Vine rather than further away. Over time, healthy buds will burst along our branches. This abundant fruit will be the byproduct of our devotion to Christ.

And we will thank God for the way He has kept us centered, grounded, and connected to Him, focused only on producing fruits that last.

Review

- The teen years provide a perfect opportunity to prepare the ground for harvest.
- The harvest we reap tomorrow will be determined by the seeds we plant today.
- To produce true, lasting, and abundant fruit, we need to remain rooted in the source of our life, love, and power—the True Vine of Christ.

Replenish

"Oh, the joys of those who do not
  follow the advice of the wicked,
  or stand around with sinners,
  or join in with mockers.
But they delight in the law of the Lord,
  meditating on it day and night.
They are like trees planted along the riverbank,
  bearing fruit each season.
Their leaves never wither,
  and they prosper in all they do"
(Psalms 1:1–3).

You who are young, make the most of your youth.
Relish your youthful vigor.
Follow the impulses of your heart.
If something looks good to you, pursue it.
But know also that not just anything goes;
You have to answer to God for every last bit of it
(Ecclesiastes 11:9 MSG).

"Don't be misled—you cannot mock the justice of God. You
will always harvest what you plant. Those who live only
to satisfy their own sinful nature will harvest decay and
death from that sinful nature. But those who live to please
the Spirit will harvest everlasting life from the Spirit"
(Galatians 6:7–8).

"Remain in me, and I will remain in you. For a branch cannot produce fruit if it is severed from the vine, and you cannot be fruitful unless you remain in me. "Yes, I am the vine; you are the branches. Those who remain in me, and I in them, will produce much fruit. For apart from me you can do nothing" (John 15:4–5).

"So let's not get tired of doing what is good. At just the right time we will reap a harvest of blessing if we don't give up" (Galatians 6:9).

Respond
Influencer Challenge

Use your sphere of influence on social media by sparking a discussion about this chapter with your friends! I challenge you to write a post that answers the following question. Be sure to use the hashtag #BecomeAnInfluencer in your response!

If you aren't on social media, no worries! You can participate in the same challenge among your friends in real life.

What are steps you can take to make the most of your youth by preparing for an eternal harvest and what exactly does this mean?

Part Five
Tapping into Your Potential

Chapter Thirteen
Fulfilling Your Purpose

R aise your hand if you're the kind of person who enjoys learning science.

If you're among the readers who didn't raise your hands, don't worry. I'm right there with you. My brain tends to operate more with its right, creative side than the left, logical side. But that doesn't mean I'm not fascinated by some of the facts I've learned about creation.

Especially the evidence that confirms the existence of a Creator.

The more I've learned, the more I've reached a conclusion: Everything God has created has a purpose for existence. His detailed, complex designs carry specific functions. Without those unique designs, life wouldn't function properly.

Take trees, for example. Where would we receive our oxygen if God didn't create them to provide us with life and to filter out harmful gasses?[46] And what about our blood? Our blood keeps us alive as well. It contains the oxygen we need and carries the oxygen from our lungs and then distributes it to our tissues and cells.[47] It accomplishes this all on its own. Talk about a complex design!

It's also interesting to realize how every living thing is dependent upon other living things for existence—humans, animals, insects, trees, etc. (Great, now I have the song "Circle of Life" stuck in my head!)

Oh, and let's not forget the way in which a woman's body was specifically designed to bear children. And how crazy is it that a mother's breast milk contains the exact amount of water, fat, sugar, and protein a baby needs to grow? If the baby becomes sick, the mother's milk will adapt for the baby's needs by providing the right antibodies to protect the baby from the specific illness.[48]

Mind-blowing, isn't it?

Last but not least, let's consider the sun and its role in providing the earth with the solar energy it needs to maintain life. If there were too little heat and energy, the earth would freeze; too much, and the earth would burn.[49]

At the risk of sounding like a textbook, I'll stop there. But with all this in mind—knowing God blueprinted a specific plan, function, and purpose for every created thing, can't we also trust He has a specific purpose and plan laid out for each of us too? And what if the unique ways He designed us can help to fulfill a specific purpose? If that's the case, then it's our responsibility to uncover this potential so we can carry out our divine calling.

Burning Passion

Can you think of a time when someone else's "success" story kindled a burning passion within you? When I was growing up, my desire to write burned greatest any time I'd hear an inspirational story about how an author achieved his or her dreams of writing. There's something about other's testimonials that ignite a fire within us to pursue what we were meant to pursue.

This is what happened to a certain college student several decades ago. He joined his theology class to visit the former home of John Wesley, a reformer of the church back in the 1700s. Wesley played a key role in bringing revival throughout England.[50] So you can imagine how inspirational it must have been for these students to visit his old home! Especially as they browsed through Wesley's former study, immersing themselves in the very books he once studied all those years ago.

But for this one college student, it wasn't the study that ignited the flame inside of him, it was Wesley's former bedroom. Or to be more specific, the spot on the carpet next to Wesley's bed—the two indentations impressed into the floor, worn from Wesley's constant kneeling as he prayed each and every morning. These two patches were evidence of the endless hours Wesley had spent praying for revival.

This enlarged the student's desire to spread the gospel so much that he couldn't seem to leave. He remained next to the bed, mesmerized, probably unaware the rest of his group had left.

While the class piled back into the bus, the professor did a head count of each student and noticed one missing. He went back through the house and searched the rooms until, finally, he found the student. He'd remained in the exact spot next to Wesley's bed. But the student was no longer standing. He was kneeling, his knees pressed into the very indentations Wesley had left behind all those centuries ago. And this student was pleading with God, "Do it again, Lord, do it again. And let it start with me."[51]

That passion burning within the student—to lead a revival—gave him the push he needed to carry out God's divine purpose for His life.

A purpose God had planned for this college student, the young Billy Graham, even before he was born.

Cocoon of Potential

Many of us may hear that story and think, "Well, he's different. God had a special calling on his life." Sure, Billy Graham may have been used to influence millions of lives for eternity, but that doesn't mean his purpose is greater than ours. Remember the Scripture about the Body of Christ and how each role carries significant value? Billy Graham's purpose may have looked more important, but the truth is, each of us has been called to do something amazing with our lives. If we fail to recognize this, then we risk missing the signs and signals God may be trying to provide us along the way. He planted potential inside of us that will help us bring our purpose into completion.

But these abilities might not be obvious at first. In fact, if you were to hear God tell you what He had in store for your life, you might shake your head and proclaim, "No way that's happening. You've got to be confusing me with someone else." Why do we have such a hard time grasping the concept God could use us in a mighty way?

Perhaps it's because our potential needs time to develop first.

You see, our calling isn't something we discover one day and jump right into the next. That's not how it worked with the characters we read about in the Bible—David, Joseph, Mary, or Moses—and it's not how it works for us either. Even Jesus Himself waited decades until He began His ministry!

There is a *transition* that must first take place within our lives.

A transition that's not too different from the one a caterpillar goes through.

In the early stages of a caterpillar's life, it doesn't look like it could amount to much, does it? From appearance, it's just another worm. And to be honest, caterpillars kind of freak me out with their hairy little bodies. (No offense to them. I'm squeamish when it comes to all types of insects.)

Other critters might be oblivious to a caterpillar's potential, but that doesn't mean the potential isn't still there. No, it might not look like much. It's hidden on the inside of the worm, integrated into the very core of its unique design. And that potential, as we all know, is to carry out its purpose to become a butterfly.

In the same way, the potential God has birthed inside of

us is integrated into the core of who we are. And it's going to help us carry out our divine purpose.

This process, however, cannot be rushed.

Can you remember what happens to a caterpillar if it's released too soon from its cocoon? If it neglects to carry out the stages of metamorphosis—which is an *active* transformation—then its wings become disfigured.[52] Its body becomes swollen. That poor almost-butterfly will never taste the freedom of spreading its wings and fulfilling its true calling.

And all because it never completed its transformation inside of the cocoon.

As sad as that sounds, I wonder how many people do the same by rushing ahead, hoping to fulfill their calling ASAP, but instead, they are unequipped, unprepared, and under-developed.

Now, here's something I don't want you to miss: Even though we might not be meant to do everything God has called us to do *immediately,* that doesn't mean we're waiting around and twiddling our thumbs.

You see, when a butterfly is developing in its cocoon, *it is never in a stage of rest.* There is much work to be done—work that's hidden from sight—as it develops its potential. This requires the shedding of its old caterpillar body and a miraculous transformation into a new creature. The wings and antennae are formed during this time. It gains the muscles and skills needed to break out of its cocoon and flourish as a butterfly.[53]

In the same way, we should never remain stagnant in our cocoon of potential. This is the time to get to work. To develop the right muscles and skills we need to fulfill our calling. To receive training to equip us for what's ahead.

And most of all, we must keep seeking God first, allowing Him to transform us into the young women He has called us to grow into. That way, when the time finally does arrive for us to break free and test out our new wings, we will be fully prepared to pursue the work He has been training us for all along.

Our True Purpose

I can remember how exciting it was for me, as a teenager, to imagine the possibilities of my future. I've always been a dreamer—it's an extension of my INFP personality. I used to imagine what it'd feel like when the time finally came for me to emerge into my divine calling. But there was one thing I needed to learn along the way:

Our true purpose isn't necessarily something we fulfill in the future. Our purpose can be carried out *today*. Because if the point of our God-given purpose is to glorify God, then why should we wait for tomorrow when we can glorify Him today?

I know you've been learning how to go about discovering your calling, but really, it doesn't have to be complicated. Our purpose is already defined for us in the Bible. It's the very reason we have been placed on this earth, and it's a calling we have the privilege of carrying out every moment of every day. And that is the call to worship God and to make His name greater.

This is what Paul meant when He wrote: *"For everything comes from him and exists by his power and is intended for his glory. All glory to him forever! Amen"* (Romans 11:36).

Yes, God created everything in creation with purpose. According to Romans 1:20, God's eternal power and divine nature is etched into every petal of the flower, painted across every stroke of the sunrise, and demonstrated through the continuous gush of every waterfall. All of creation was created with the intention of pointing back to the Creator, and everything that has breath has been destined to praise the Lord (Psalm 150:6).

That's why the quest to fulfill our purpose doesn't need to be complicated. Actually, it's this very divine purpose in our lives—to glorify God—that should spur us into embracing the adventure of discovering our assignment and preparing accordingly. Our purpose should be an extension of our call to worship, to do everything unto the glory of the Lord (Colossians 3:23–24), and to carry His name throughout the ends of the earth.

Are you ready to continue along your journey of transformation? I believe God wants to use you in a mighty way. Perhaps it's time for you to believe that as well. Perhaps it's time for you to view yourself as a young woman who is being trained, equipped, and molded, preparing for a wonderful calling. A calling that will require you to use your gifts as an offering of worship unto Him.

And that alone should be the true drive behind fulfilling our purpose.

Chapter Fourteen
Your Role in God's Story

The other day I was reading a book by my favorite novelist, an author who has been dubbed as the "queen of Christian fiction" by *Time* magazine, and I came across one of the most emotional scenes I've ever read. It played out like a movie in my mind. It was like I was right there in the scenes, experiencing the grief of the characters as they lost their loved one.

I didn't just get teary-eyed like I usually do while reading a book that tugs on my heart strings. I wept. I had to grab tissues and take a breather and put the book down as I reminded myself it was only a story and the characters weren't real.

But part of me couldn't accept that. I knew, even though the story and characters might be fictional, they still represented real people. Real experiences. Real emotions that arise when we lose someone we love. And this story in particular featured a soldier who had risked his life for the country he loved—which was partly why it was too hard to accept it was fiction. Because the loss of his fictional life represented the true losses of young men and women who have sacrificed their lives for my country. Several days passed before I had the emotional energy to pick the book up again and continue.

Why do stories affect us like this? For centuries, humans have written them, acted in them, shared them around a campfire, read books to their children at bedtime, and watched stories play out on the screens or in theaters. It brings people together and helps them feel a sense of belonging and purpose.

Trust me, as both an author of fiction and an actress, I have spent countless hours studying the craft and structure of storytelling. I understand the power they contain to enlighten us with the truth. Isn't that why Jesus often shared spiritual concepts in the guise of parables? The characters we read about in books or watch in movies help us feel a sense of connection, especially when they can serve as a mirror for our own lives.

And yet it's not just about the entertainment factor. You see, I believe stories are written into the very fabric of our human nature. We resonate with them so deeply because we are all a part of the grand story of life the Creator has written. The theme of good conquering evil is integrated into the DNA of the gospel. Perhaps the reason we root for characters to grow as they face opposition is because we, too, have been created to conquer.

The "characters" in the story of the gospel, which includes

all of us, were created to push back the dark forces of evil and usher in the light of God's kingdom. All for the purpose of preparing for the happy ending: When Jesus Christ returns, and the Enemy will be defeated, once and for all.

But the choice of whether we will step into this important role is up to us. So what does this mean practically speaking?

An Attack on a Dream

At thirteen years old, a surfer from Hawaii by the name of Bethany Hamilton received international attention—although it wasn't necessarily because of her talent as a surfer. It was because of a shark attack that left her with only one arm.

You may have heard her story before. It's been shared across numerous outlets, portrayed in both a Hollywood film and a documentary and written about in her autobiographical book titled *Soul Surfer*. This is a true inspirational story about how one girl refused to allow an obstacle to keep her from pursuing her God-given dream to become a surfer. Even though she nearly lost her life when a fourteen-foot tiger shark attacked her, she refused to allow the traumatic impact of the event to scare her away from getting back in the water.

Besides, it wasn't the loss of an arm that devastated her the most. It was the loss of her surfing aspirations. This is a girl who, growing up in Hawaii, had lived and breathed the sport for as long as she could remember. She learned how to ride the waves at the ripe age of three and then spent nearly every day out in the sunlit water, harnessing her craft. She was only eight years old when she entered the competition world, and at the time of the attack, it seemed as though her entire life would be devoted to surfing.[54]

So it's no wonder this shark attack felt like an attack on her dreams as well!

Many people in her shoes would have looked at the one arm and said, "Oh, well. I guess I have no choice but to find a new passion." Bethany, however, possessed traits we all must develop if we hope to pursue our gifts. First, she knew, with God, anything was possible. Second, she had a stubborn determination to pursue her passion. Nothing could get in her way.

These traits spurred her to get back into the water as soon as she could. Twenty-six days after the shark bite, Bethany did just that. She continued to embrace new challenges when she entered her first major competition less than three months after the attack.

Talk about determination!

On her blog, Bethany explains why she continued to pursue her surfing dream:

When we rock the things we are naturally good at, or pursue the good things that make us excited, I believe we are honoring God. Surfing has been one of my passions for most of my life and that is why it was a given for me that I would get back on the board at the age of 13 after I lost my arm. As I've said many times, I was more afraid of losing surfing than I was of getting back in the water....

God gave me my love for the ocean and I honor him when I delight in that passion.[55]

Bethany's response to this obstacle is what eventually enabled her to touch millions of lives. People from all over the world have been inspired by her reliance on God's strength, and they, too, are motivated to do the same when facing their own challenges and setbacks.

Maybe the reason stories like Bethany's resonate with us in this manner—the reason we adore stories that feature characters who grow in the face of challenges—is because we, too, have been created to conquer.

Created to Conquer

I've had the opportunity to edit and review multiple fiction manuscripts throughout the years as part of my job in the publishing industry. When I do this, there are a few questions I must ask myself—and one of the most important questions concerns the growth of the main character. If the main character faces conflict and yet he or she doesn't grow as a result, then the character comes across as weak. The story becomes dull.

No one wants to read about a character who can't overcome adversity. And no one wants to reach the ending of a story, only to discover the bad guys won.

Think about how different the *Spider-Man* stories would be if Peter Parker never used his special powers to fight against crime. But there's a reason these Marvel movies have kept a large audience for decades. Deep inside of us is a desire to become a superhero as well. Okay, so maybe not the kind of superhero that fights against evil goblins and weird octopus creatures, but the type of heroes who can face opposition in life and grow stronger as a result.

We find pleasure in witnessing good triumph over evil.

That's because we, too, have been designed to overcome the hardships of life. Sports injuries. The loss of a loved one. A virus that sweeps over the entire world and alters our previous reality.

Yes, the sting of suffering is real. There's no denying that. But there is also no denying the *greater* reality of God's death-defeating power abiding within us. The work Jesus accomplished for us on the cross is the reason we no longer need to be beaten down by sin and suffering. Paul wrote the following truth in Romans 8:31 and v. 37: *"What shall we say about such wonderful things as these? If God is for us, who can ever be against us?...No, despite all these things, overwhelming victory is ours through Christ, who loved us."*

The Enemy is going to do his best to kick us down. And once we're down, he's going to strive to keep us there. It's in those moments when we need to do as Bethany Hamilton did and rely on God's strength in our weaknesses to pull us out of the pits.

That's another thing I love about stories: *It's the conflict that makes those happy endings so much sweeter.* In fact, a story simply wouldn't be the same without the conflict and the way the characters grow in the face of opposition.

Think about the story of Joseph in the Bible (Genesis 37-50). His own brothers sold him into slavery! As if that wasn't bad enough, Pharaoh ended up accusing Joseph of doing something he didn't do, and Joseph became locked in prison for years as punishment.

He could've raised his fists at God during this time. Who knows? Maybe he did for a day or two. But Joseph's strong faith in God seems to be what pulled him through.

Years later, Joseph was promoted to a position of power in Egypt. In this new role he carried out his divine responsibility as influencer. And when he reconciled with his brothers, he said something we can all learn from: *"You intended to harm me, but God intended it all for good. He brought me to this position so I could save the lives of many people"* (Genesis 50:20).

The opposition we face in life can result in lasting harm—if we allow it to fester.

Or it can result in the saving of lives—*if we allow it.*

Bethany Hamilton is one example of someone who chose the latter. In the 2011 movie *Soul Surfer,* a story inspired by her attack, Bethany's character says this in the film: "I wouldn't change what happened to me because then I wouldn't have this chance, in front of all of you, to embrace more people than I ever could have with two arms."

We were created to conquer.

It's in the overcoming we grow into who God has called us to become. And as we grow into who God has called us to become, we increase our potential to be used as influencers.

The Significance of Your Role

There's something else I evaluate when I edit manuscripts, and that involves the characters. I must analyze each one and ask myself, "Did this character play an important role in the story?" If the answer is "no," then I must deliver this sad news to the author. I must tell them their story would be far stronger if the character was cut out.

Every character must serve a significant purpose in some way. Good authors understand this technique. So don't you think the Author of Life grasps this concept as well? Don't you know He has planned for you to make a significant contribution to the overall story of the gospel?

But like everything in life, we have a choice. We have been given free will. And just because God has already written our life story doesn't mean we won't face tragedies and hardships.

Whether or not we use these obstacles to grow is up to us. If we do choose to grow from these conflicts, then God can do His job and accomplish good from it, just like Paul wrote about in Romans 8:28: *"And we know that God causes everything to work together for the good of those who love God and are called according to his purpose for them."*

Maybe you feel like you've made too many mistakes for God to use you. Or maybe you think you have too many flaws that could get in the way. But can I remind you that Author God has the tendency to use the weak, broken, and imperfect people for the purpose of spreading His glory?

Moses stuttered, but God chose him to lead His people to the Promised Land. Saul used to behead Christians, and yet God transformed him into Paul and he played a significant role in spreading the gospel. The woman at the well was living with a man who wasn't her husband, and yet she was chosen to become the first influencer for Jesus.

Let's not place limits on the role God has designed for us to step into. Because if the Author of Life didn't plan for us to advance the kingdom in some way, then I truly believe He wouldn't have gone through the trouble of creating us. And according to Ephesians 2:10, we can trust *"we are God's masterpiece. He has created us anew in Christ Jesus, so we can do the good things he planned for us long ago."*

Did you hear that? *We have been created to do good things.* Works that can help to spread the gospel, glorify God, and love other people. This is what our role in God's grand story involves. These are the plans He has prepared us for; it is the story He has written on our lives, as David describes in Psalm 139:16: *"You saw me before I was born. Every day of my life was recorded in your book. Every moment was laid out before a single day had passed."*

I want to leave you with two final questions:

Are you ready to embrace this unique role God has designed for you to fulfill?

Are you ready to serve your significant role in advancing His kingdom?

I hope your answer is yes. I'd hate for the grand story of the gospel to miss out on your role's significant contribution!

Chapter Fifteen
Unleash Your Strengths

We're all aware of the damage that resulted from COVID in 2020. I don't need to remind you of the negative changes it may have introduced to your life, but if we dig deep enough, we might find a few positive changes this pandemic introduced into our lives as well:

Such as the opportunity to spend more time with our loved ones during the lockdown. (Although you may not believe spending extra time with your brother should be labeled a "positive change.")

An appreciation for the small things in life. Like seeing an actual human being while going for a walk.

More free time to discover new hobbies. Even if this "new hobby" involved making TikTok videos.

One of the positive changes that lockdown introduced to my life was a new discipline I integrated into my daily routine. The discipline of working out on a consistent basis.

Might sound ironic since the gyms were closed during the lockdown, but I guess you could say remaining in the house for so long made me somewhat stir crazy. I had too much energy that needed to be released *somehow*.

That's when my cousin introduced me to a virtual training workout app that offers a variety of classes. I became hooked. These classes offered a much-needed release for me, and the more muscles I built during this time, the stronger I became, and the more advanced classes I was able to take.

However, it took time for these muscles to develop. Fortunately, time was something I didn't lack during the lockdown! This strength wasn't built overnight. But if I had never integrated workouts into my daily routine—if I had remained stagnant, settling for the comfortable—then I never would've witnessed what I was capable of.

You see, it is only by challenging myself that I tapped into my true potential. I needed to push my limits so I could grow.

This is a lesson we can apply to every aspect of our life— not just in working out.

Why do we often hold ourselves back from discovering our potential? Why do we think we must be born as a talented professional with a specific gift or skill? Sure, we may be born with a certain talent, but like anything else in life, those talented muscles must be sharpened.

The same applies to our brain as well. Yes, God has given each of us a brain. But if we never sharpened our brain with mental exercises, then it'd remain underdeveloped, and we would never discover our true potential.

God never called us to remain stagnant. No, not even

during a lockdown! He has gifted us with talents and skills for a reason, but it's our decision whether we will develop them into their fullest capacity. This growth can only occur when we embrace the challenging and not-so-comfortable opportunities that push our "specialties" to their limits. If you can learn how to do this now, as a teenager, I believe you might even surprise yourself with the muscles you'll develop!

It Begins With Belief

There are some dreams that may seem completely out of reach because of the odds stacked against us. For a kid named Michael Oher, his dream of becoming an NFL football player seemed impossible. Not necessarily because he wasn't athletic enough; after all, he had always been a big guy for his age.

Rather, it was because he grew up in an environment prone to grooming kids to join gangs and become drug addicts. This could have easily been the life Michael Oher settled for, especially since he didn't have a stable home environment.

But being a gang member was not Michael's aspiration. In fact, in an interview with ABC News in 2009, he claims to have *intentionally made the decision* he was going to be somebody.[56]

This decision is what ultimately spurred him to work hard academically and to achieve good grades.

Before he made this decision, however, he didn't have much of a reason to try hard in school. Michael was adopted into a loving family in high school, but before then, his lack of effort in school resulted in poor grades and a .06 GPA level. One year, he was absent from school a total of fifty-one times. It's no wonder his grades were suffering! His education never had a chance to develop.[57]

It wasn't until Michael was adopted and enrolled in a Christian school that he had the support system he needed to thrive. What was his motivation for increasing his GPA? His dream of becoming an NFL player. After all, he would never receive a college football scholarship with the grades he had previously been making.[58]

Michael said every morning he would wake up and tell himself he was going to work hard to get to that next level.[59] No, it didn't come naturally. At sixteen years old, Michael didn't even know what a verb or a noun was. He had to be tutored outside of his traditional classes and take oral exams rather than written exams because of his difficulties.[60]

But over time—with consistent effort to improve himself academically and embrace new challenges—Michael finally improved his grades.

It all began with his belief. He chose to believe that he could, in his words, "be somebody."

And it's his belief that spurred him into action.

Because if he had not made the decision to rise to the next level, then he never would've reached his dream of becoming an NFL player for the Baltimore Ravens. How tragic that would have been! Not only could he have potentially settled for the life of poverty, gangs, and addiction—the lifestyle he was surrounded by in his childhood—but he also never would've touched millions of lives when his story became dramatized in the Hollywood film *The Blind Side.*

In Michael's book, *I Beat the Odds,* he shares his experience about how he unleashed his potential to improve academically. The secret? He had to first believe it was possible. He said, "People like to talk about 'Cinderella stories,' but Cinderella didn't get her happy ending without lifting a finger. She had to show up at the ball, be charming and smooth, and win over the prince. Of course she had help along the way, but ultimately it was up to her to make the fairy-tale ending happen."[61]

Breaking Free from the Ropes

Stepping into our God-given calling involves breaking free from the barriers tied around our abilities. It's like the story about the man at an elephant camp who noticed the elephants weren't held back by cages or chains. Have you heard this story before? Even though these elephants didn't have cages or chains to hold them back, they were still confined in a tiny area.

The only thing that held them back were small ropes tied to their legs.

Upon seeing this, the man wondered, "Why aren't the elephants breaking free from those ropes? Surely they know how powerful and strong they are!" He asked the elephant trainer why the elephants didn't try to break free. The trainer's response? "They don't know they can. We used those ropes to hold them back when they were baby elephants, and back then, they could never break free. As time passed and they grew older and stronger, they never tried again. They were conditioned, from a young age, to believe that they were confined by this rope."[62]

Wow! These large elephants neglected to recognize their own potential and strength. It's because of their lack of belief that they never overcame those barriers and unleashed their strength to break free.

Now, I don't think that actually occurred in real life—but isn't that an accurate reflection of how some people spend their lives? God didn't create us to remain confined. He gifted us with the strength we need to break free from strongholds, embrace our potential, and pursue our calling. But, as we have already discussed, it all begins with our belief.

Many of the most successful people in life aren't the ones who were born into wealth; rather, they're the ones who refused to believe they *couldn't* attain success. They chose not to allow the ropes to hold them back.

Why, then, should we, as children of God, confine ourselves to the limitations in our lives? Why do we often make excuses as to why we shouldn't carry out our role as influencer? "I can't share the gospel to a stranger. I'm an introvert." Or "I'm from a small town and come from an average family. Who am I to think God can use someone like me to make a significant impact on this world?"

If we hope to become all God has called us to be, touching lives He has called us to touch, then we must first believe we are capable. God *can* use us, no matter our personality, appearance, or social status. And that belief should spur us into action.

Action involves sharpening our skills, like Michael Oher had to do. It involves embracing new challenges that might terrify us at first. Challenges that stretch our known capacity or perhaps even seem impossible. But how else is our strength going to reach its potential if it's never given the opportunity to be unleashed? If we don't at least try to sharpen our gifts, then we're always going to remain stagnant, like those elephants. We'll remain confined in one area, blind to the power God has gifted us with.

Thomas Edison is credited to have said this truth: "If we did all the things we are capable of, we would literally astound ourselves."[63] He was quite an intelligent man, wouldn't you agree? That's why I must believe he knew what he was talking about.

Helen Keller is a good example of someone who applied this wisdom—whether she did it intentionally or not. She could've easily allowed her deafness and blindness to hold her back from excelling in academics and in life; instead, she devoted hard work into breaking free from her "ropes." Her perseverance eventually caused her to become the first deaf and blind person to earn a Bachelor of Arts degree.[64]

This is an achievement many would have deemed as impossible. But Helen Keller wasn't going to settle for the average life, allowing her disabilities to keep her confined. God created her with unique potential to make a difference, like He did with each of us, but she had to believe she was capable of more. She had to refuse to view those ropes as limitations. Perhaps that's what she meant when she said, "It's a terrible thing to see and have no vision." It's because of her vision—to view herself as someone who could achieve—that she manifested her belief into action. She became an author, an activist, and a speaker who helped millions of lives and whose legacy continues to make a difference.[65]

Let's decide today to rewire our minds and view our own

limitations as "ropes around our ankles" rather than true strongholds. Then there will be no limits on how God can use us to accomplish the seemingly impossible!

Don't Quit The Membership

Maybe you have experienced the exhilaration that comes after building muscles—whether it's resulted from working out or participating in sports. It's nice to see progress and to feel stronger, especially after devoting hours of hard work into a certain discipline, don't you think?

But we often don't feel too motivated while doing that first exercise. Especially if it's been a while since our muscles were strengthened. It's tiring to face new growth opportunities, pushing our limits, and exhausting our physical strength. That exhaustion, along with the lack of immediate results from our efforts, is why many people neglect to keep a consistent workout routine. It helps to explain why January is the busiest month for most gyms: People have good intentions to get in shape. Their goal for the new year is to create a habit of working out. To lose unnecessary weight.

Yet once February rolls around and those people haven't already grown into Muscle Man or Woman, they decide it's no longer worth it, and they quit their gym memberships. I don't want you to be the kind of person to quit your membership, figuratively speaking. Obviously I'm not referring to strengthening yourself physically (unless that's what you feel called to do); rather, this applies to strengthening the unique gifts and skills God has given us. As with working out, one of the main reasons people fail to unleash their potential is because they never see immediate results. And why is that? Because those results are not quick. Muscles take time to develop. It is only through consistent, every-day effort—devoting intentional time toward sharpening a certain skill—we will soon become whipped into shape. Yes, we may grow weary in the process. Especially on days when we simply don't feel equipped for the task. But if challenges were meant to be easy, then they wouldn't be known as *challenges,* now, would they?

Popular businessman and entrepreneur, Jeff Olson, says in his bestselling book *The Slight Edge,* "Any time you see what looks like a breakthrough, it is always the end result of a long series of little things, done consistently over time."[66]

The point is, as we do series of little things, *we don't have to be perfect.* It's okay to falter and stumble, especially as we're taking those baby steps. God isn't calling us to perfection; He is calling us to diligence. To make the most of what He has placed inside of us and to do everything for His glory alone (Colossians 3:23; 1 Corinthians 10:31). He's not going to force us to discover what we could become.

That hard part is up to us. But we're never going to know what lies within us until we try. Until we take those courses. Practice. Experiment. Set challenges that might intimidate us, goals that stretch ourselves a little.

Those challenging obstacles that may have kept you stuck in place are ropes, not chains. And the God who abides within you is far more powerful than those limitations. Limitations such as laziness. Fear of rejection, failure, or men's approval. Perfection paralysis—the inability to work because we feel like we must be the *best,* or else we shouldn't pursue it. False humility. And any other lies from the Enemy.

Because with God's help, you *can* make it past those strongholds and step into the breakthrough of your calling.

Michael Oher said it perfectly in his book, *I Beat the Odds:* "You are a unique person created for a specific purpose. Your gifts matter. Your story matters. Your dreams matter. You matter."[67]

God chose you to be on this earth at this time in history to make a difference that only you can make.

I believe in you. I believe you can unleash your power and potential. But, you see, my belief alone isn't enough to spur you into action. The question that will matter in the long run is this:

Do *you* believe that you can?

Review

- God designed us in a way that can help us carry out our life's purpose—and the *purpose of our purpose* is to glorify God.

- We can step into the unique role God has created for us, playing a part in the grand story of the gospel.

- It's our responsibility to unleash our potential and sharpen our skills so they can be used for God's kingdom.

Replenish

"For everything comes from him and exists by his power and is intended for his glory. All glory to him forever! Amen" (Romans 11:36).

"You saw me before I was born. Every day of my life was recorded in your book. Every moment was laid out before a single day had passed" (Psalm 139:16).

"Work willingly at whatever you do, as though you were working for the Lord rather than for people" (Colossians 3:23).

"Come, all of you who are gifted craftsmen. Construct everything that the Lord has commanded" (Exodus 35:10).

" In his grace, God has given us different gifts for doing certain things well. So if God has given you the ability to prophesy, speak out with as much faith as God has given you. If your gift is serving others, serve them well. If you are a teacher, teach well. If your gift is to encourage others, be encouraging. If it is giving, give generously. If God has given you leadership ability, take the responsibility seriously. And if you have a gift for showing kindness to others, do it gladly" (Romans 12:6–8).

Respond
Influencer Challenge

Use your sphere of influence on social media by sparking a discussion about this chapter with your friends! I challenge you to write a post that answers the following question. Be sure to use the hashtag #BecomeAnInfluencer in your response!

If you aren't on social media, no worries! You can participate in the same challenge among your friends in real life.

**What would you recommend for you and your peers
to excel in your gifts so you can make a difference?**

Part Six

Making a Difference Today, Not Tomorrow

Chapter Sixteen
There Is No Age Requirement

Have you ever wondered what it would be like to be ageless? Rather than growing another year older on your birthday, you would remain the same age you are at this very moment. Maybe that would be exciting at first, but I'm sure it'd get redundant eventually, don't you think?

This was the premise of a movie I recently watched, *Age of Adeline*. When Adeline was around thirty years old, she had a car accident that magically jolted her brain, causing her to remain at her current age. *Forever.* The movie is based on a true story. (Okay, I'm only joking about that part!)

Even though, unlike Adeline, I continue to age year after year, I still feel like I can relate with her. Sometimes it seems as if time has frozen and kept me young forever. Perhaps partly because I am frequently mistaken as a teenager by strangers, and also since I'm the youngest in my family—including the youngest of thirteen cousins. When I was a kid,

I yearned to have respect in the eyes of my older sisters and cousins. I didn't want to be seen as an immature child. I kept waiting for my age to grant me this feeling of respect—but that moment never arrived. And I've finally realized why:

Because, no matter how old I become, I will always be the "baby" of the family.

There's another factor that played into me feeling forever young. When I first started teaching at writing conferences, I was always the youngest on the faculty. My quiet demeanor, along with being short in stature, didn't help my attempts to appear mature. The conference attendees often assumed I was about ten years younger than I was.

Now, don't get me wrong—it's a compliment to be told I look younger than I am! But what bothers me is when young people are disrespected because of their age. As if God doesn't use young people before they have gained decades of life experience and wisdom. As if Jesus Himself didn't tell His disciples in Matthew 18:3 to "become like little children."

Sometimes I wonder if God created me "forever young" on purpose; that way, I don't attempt to rely on my appearance, age, voice, height, or whatever else to grant me confidence; instead, He wants me to ground my confidence in Him. To strive to impress people with the light inside of me, despite my age.

I believe He wants the same for you as well.

You don't need to wait until you have decades of life experience or a certain number of degrees under your belt before you can make a difference. From the beginning of time, God has used people of all ages to accomplish His purposes on earth.

So what will it look like for you to make a difference today, despite your age, rather than waiting for tomorrow?

Why Wait?

I attended my first writing conference when I was sixteen years old. At this conference, attendees had the opportunity to pitch their books to professionals in the publishing world to be considered for publication. They also made appointments to meet with the authors on faculty to receive fifteen minutes of mentorship.

I was thrilled to have this opportunity, especially since this was the first conference I had ever attended. The author I chose to meet with wrote teen fiction, so I thought she'd be the perfect person to receive advice from as a teen writer.

But the appointment didn't go as I had planned it.

Now, this is a lovely lady and in no way do I hold resentment toward her for this experience. But sadly, as soon as I sat down with her—before I could speak a word or show her my writing samples—she said, "Before you show me anything, I just want to tell you that I always advise teens to wait until they're in their late twenties before pursuing publication." And then she proceeded to explain her reasoning behind this advice: Many teens only become published *because* of their age. Then, once their book becomes a one-hit-wonder, they never make a true career out of writing. They also don't have enough life experience to write yet.

I completely understood where she was coming from. But it's a good thing I didn't follow this advice—otherwise, I would *just now* be pursuing publication for the first time.

Again, in no way do I hold resentment toward this author. But I can't help but wonder—*why?* Why do adults often not believe God can use young people? That they need to wait until they've collected more life experience and education before pursuing their calling? Why do people think there is one right way for *everyone* when God has written a different story for each of us?

It is true that both experience and education contribute to helping us become well-rounded individuals. They can certainly play an important factor in our calling as well. Yet at the same time, we must remember God uses different measurements of judgment than we do. Just ask King David.

Can you remember the Bible story about how he was first anointed as king? Before God brought him into this position, he was a young, humble shepherd—the youngest of seven sons. When he was a teen, God instructed a man named Samuel to visit the home of Jesse, David's father, because He wanted Samuel to anoint one of Jesse's sons to become king.

When Jesse first arrived, he met all the sons. ...well, all except David since he was out in the fields. At first, Samuel automatically assumed Eliab was the one God wanted to anoint. Why? Because Samuel was judging from a human standpoint. After he said, *"Surely this is the Lord's anointed!"* (1 Samuel 16:6)—referring to Eliab—God was quick to correct him. *"But the Lord said to Samuel, 'Don't judge by his appearance or height, for I have rejected him. The Lord doesn't see things the way you see them. People judge by outward appearance, but the Lord looks at the heart'"* (v. 7).

So Jesse proceeded to present Samuel with his other sons.

And each time he met one, Samuel knew that son was not the one the Lord had anointed to become the king of Israel.

After Jesse had presented him with the remaining sons, Samuel seemed a little confused. He knew none of these sons were God's chosen one. That's because the one God had anointed, David, was still out in the fields.

Get this: Jesse, David's own father, didn't even consider David to be an option. He apparently didn't deem David worthy enough to even be presented to Samuel as a possible king.

Ouch! Talk about rejection from your own father.

Finally, Samuel asked Jesse (v. 11), *"Are these all the sons you have?"*

And then Jesse admitted he had another son. Upon hearing this, Samuel requested for Jesse to bring David to him. As soon as Samuel laid eyes on David, God spoke to him, telling him he was the one to be anointed as king.

Isn't it interesting how God didn't wait for David to grow up first? He didn't wait for him to become a man who would be wealthier in terms of experience, wisdom, or intelligence. Nor did he choose David's older brothers to be king, even though they seemed to fit the bill—from a human standpoint, at least.

Instead, God wanted to use David, *because of his youthfulness.* And it's from David's family line the Messiah would one day arrive.

This is just one of many Bible stories that demonstrates how God uses young people to further His kingdom. If He doesn't think young people should wait before carrying out His purposes, then why should we?

Why should you wait if God is wanting to use you *today* rather than tomorrow?

Anointing Trumps Age

The room was packed with almost one hundred people, most of whom were at least fifteen years older than I was. I was at another writing conference, only this time I was in my mid-twenties rather than a teen, and I wasn't preparing for an appointment with an author as I had been when I was sixteen. I was preparing to share the morning devotion before this group.

I hadn't expected so many people to attend this meeting. In addition, I could hardly sleep the night before because I was so nervous. I had spoken at conferences numerous times, but those were writing workshops. For some reason, this felt different. Like I was in the spotlight. But I did my best to mask my nerves. I wore my best smile as I took confident strides to the podium, silently asking the Holy Spirit to flow through me.

As I started to speak, He did exactly that. My message was about how we were created to both worship God and to create, and how we can fulfill both when we worship God through our creations. My passion for sharing this message soon overshadowed the nerves. It wasn't about me; rather, it was about sharing the message I felt God had placed on my heart.

Fortunately, it must have been received well, too, because a few people approached to thank me afterward. The last lady to approach me said, "I owe you an apology."

Of course, this statement caught me off guard. I had never even met her before, after all!

She continued and said, "When you first walked up to the podium, I was thinking, 'There's nothing I could learn from this sixteen-year-old.' But I was proven wrong."

Why do I share this story with you? Not to pat myself on the back (after all, I would *never* have the guts to speak if God didn't help me in my weakness!). But to show you how, very often, our judgment as humans differs from God's. We can't see from His vantage-point. He has stepped outside of time. Who knows, God could even be watching the scene from the Garden of Eden unfold while you are reading this book! He knows every detail about the moment you were born, and He knows every detail about your future as well.

Remember the caterpillar-to-butterfly analogy I shared with you in chapter thirteen? Well, when we're young, people may see us as that little caterpillar, crawling through the grass, because they're blind to the potential God placed inside of us to grow into that butterfly.

I wonder if this explains why God, throughout the Bible, instructed us to live to please Him rather than humans. Not only is fearing people a form of idol worship, but it can hold us back from living the life God has called us to live.

For example, let's say you feel compelled to audition for the worship band at your church. You've surrendered this desire to God in your prayer time, evaluated your heart to confirm this desire is to make *His* name greater rather than your own. And still, that desire has only grown into a flame of burning passion. The Holy Spirit inside of you confirms this is what you were meant to do.

You present this idea to some of the mentors in your life. After all, God often uses our mentors—especially our parents or guardians—to speak truth into our lives. And even though there are some adults who may be on board with your decision to audition for the worship band, maybe one person isn't sold. Why? Because he or she believes you need time to mature. Not just your music and singing skills, but also your character. This person tells you this position would only go to your head, and you may not be spiritually mature enough to handle the spotlight.

What do you do with feedback like this? I first suggest, once again, surrendering it to God. Ask Him to reveal if He was speaking through that person—if that person has given you biblical advice you should heed—or if he or she was simply judging from their human standpoint.

Because the thing is, we're all human. And we're all tempted to give a false judgment from our human perceptions, even when we think we're being wise.

There may come a time when you, as a young person, experience rejection and resistance from adults—possibly even from your loved ones. It's natural for those who have greater experience and education to believe they know what's best. And don't get me wrong: *Most of the time, they do.* Especially mentors and parents who offer biblically-sound wisdom regarding your life choices. So in no way am I advising you to rebel against the authority God has placed in your life! Yet when it comes down to it, we are called to obey God rather than men. If an authority figure were to advise you to steal a dress from a boutique, would you give in? Of course not! To do so would be to directly violate God and His Word.

In the same way, I believe we are to obey God when it comes to *every* area of our lives. Only He can see us for who we truly are. He knows how He has designed us to make a difference for His kingdom. The anointing we receive from Him will trump age every time—just like it did with David. And if God is calling you to take a leap of faith as a young person, then He must have a good reason for doing so.

"Don't Let Anyone Think Less of You"

There's someone else in the Bible who received criticism because of his age. This young person, Timothy, stepped into the position as a leader of the church in Ephesus, but naturally, there were those who weren't afraid of voicing their opinions about his age. Paul encouraged him with these words: *"Don't let anyone think less of you because you are young. Be an example to all believers in what you say, in the way you live, in your love, your faith, and your purity"* (1 Timothy 4:12). The NIV translation phrases the first sentence as, *"Don't let anyone look down on you."*

Think about that for a moment. If Paul is encouraging Timothy to refuse to allow others to think less of him, that must mean Timothy had a *choice.* It would've been easy for him to allow the judgments and opinions of others to hold him back, to keep him from moving forward in the position God had granted him. But since Timothy couldn't gain respect with his age and experience, Paul challenged him to gain respect by the examples he set instead.

An example in his speech, his life, his love, his faith, and his purity.

Paul encouraged Timothy to be an influencer for God's kingdom in all these areas. To reflect the light of Christ through his spiritual maturity—a maturity that has nothing to do with age nor experience.

Because in God's kingdom, *there is no age requirement.* The only requirement we are given is to love God and others (Matthew 22:36–40), and to devote our lives into spreading the gospel (Matthew 28:19–20). How? By allowing Christ to shine through our speech, our life, our love, our faith, and our purity.

That alone is *true* maturity.

And it's this maturity that will capture the attention of those around us. This isn't something we should strive to do so others can praise us for the light radiating from us; rather, when they see us shining, they should be compelled to see Christ *behind* the light.

So I want to leave you with the same challenge Paul presented to Timothy in his letter:

Will you refuse to allow the rejection and resistance from others to hold you back from making a difference *today* rather than just waiting for tomorrow? Will you turn your eyes away from your lack and focus your gaze on your source of Christ instead?

Then, the reason people will become impressed by you is not because of your age, education, experience, or qualification. In fact, gaining respect from other people should never be our goal in the first place. Instead, when you shine, people will be compelled to admire how great, mighty, and powerful our God is. So great He has chosen to use people of all ages to further His ministry on earth.

Yes, even teenagers.

Chapter Seventeen
Your Sphere of Influence

I don't know if you read fiction or not, but if you do, doesn't it frustrate you when a teen novel features unrealistic teen characters? I had an issue with this when I was a teen myself. There were some contemporary fiction books I read that were cringe-worthy because the youth culture looked nothing like the one I was immersed in. It also frustrated me when the author seemed to "look down" on teens by the way they were portrayed. As though they were far younger and more immature than they were in real life.

This is one reason why I wanted to write a teen fiction novel while I was still a teen myself, because I had tasted firsthand the bitter emotions of teen angst. I knew how the pressures of the culture played a significant role in developing body image issues among teens. Every week I heard classmates vent about their home life.

There's a difference between merely recalling the teen

experiences and emotions—like I'm doing right now—and actually being in the midst of them.

This helps explain why many readers connected to the main character in my first novel, *Purple Moon*—the book I wrote when I was sixteen. Because the voice authentically reflected a teenager, and the struggles she faced were based on real-life issues modern-day teens experienced.

I understood because I could relate. And it's because of being able to relate I was then able to connect with my peers on a deep level.

For some reason, when we experience hard things in life, it's often tough for us to open our ears to hear from someone who can't relate. You know what I mean? That's why we often say those words, "You just don't understand."

But what about when we receive counsel from someone who *does* understand? Someone who has also experienced the trauma of losing a loved one or has felt the pain of heartbreak from a breakup? Then we seem to be more attentive to what that person has to say.

You, as a teen, may be able to reach your peers on a deeper level than I can. Who better to make an impact on them than someone who is around them daily?

No, you don't need to wait until you grow older; in fact, it might be too late if you do that! So what can you do today that could bring a positive impact on your sphere of influence?

Be the Change

I was fifteen years old when I attended a church youth camp

and was introduced to the story of Zach Hunter. I watched from my seat in the large auditorium—an auditorium that housed thousands of students—as this teenager gave the story about how he launched his campaign at only twelve years old. A campaign called Loose Change to Loosen Chains that fought against modern-day slavery.

This captivated me. How could a guy who was around my age make such an impact on a social injustice issue? This campaign had gone on to donate millions of dollars toward the abolition movement. Not only was Zach making a difference for those affected by modern-day slavery, but here he was, standing before thousands of teens, encouraging them to make a difference as well.

Age didn't hold him back from doing something about slavery. It all started when Zach was learning about Harriet Tubman in school—the woman who led the Underground Railroad. As he heard about her story, he said to his mom, "Man, if I had lived back then, I would have fought for equality, and against slavery."[68] That's when she told him slavery still occurred today. The oppression just took on a different shape and form.

Zach became convinced he had to do something about this. But his father reminded him of his age, telling him it may prevent him from doing anything. Still, he couldn't ignore the urge God had given him to fight against this injustice. What would be the purpose in waiting?[69]

Since Zach launched his campaign, he has also published numerous books—such as *Generation Change* and *Be the Change*—in which he inspires other teens to make a difference as well.

And those teens, including myself back then, were attentive to what he had to say. Why? Because he had proven it was possible to make a difference. It was possible to be a teenager and, at the same time, follow that burning passion in his heart. The passion that compelled him to shed God's light and love in some way.

That's exactly what happened to me as I sat in the auditorium, watching Zach Hunter share his story three years after he launched his campaign. A fire lit up within me. Because I wanted to be used as well. I wanted God to use me then, as a teenager, and not just in my future.

In a YouTube video filmed when he was a teen, Zach said, "I think that we [our generation] can even have sort of this new peace and love movement. Except instead of what the hippies try to do without God, you know, we can try to do it *with* God."[70]

If every teenager today would use their voice to bring God's peace and love to the lives and circumstances around them, think about the shift that would occur within this generation!

Igniting Your Small Flame

I can't help but wonder—what if Zach Hunter had talked himself out of starting his cause? Let's think about the reasons why he could've excused himself from making this change.

First, he could have believed he was too young, too unqualified, to make a difference.

Second, he could have seen himself as too small to truly make a change in such a large issue as modern-day slavery.

And third, he could've waited until he received multiple confirmations from God before he took that first step. As though God needed to speak to Zach in a booming voice to spur him into action.

But he didn't allow any of those potential excuses to hold him back.

In the books Zach has written, as well as the interviews with him, he explains why we don't need to wait when it comes to making a difference. Because if there is a passion in our hearts—for example, to fight for injustice—and it aligns with God's Word, then we can be assured that it is, in fact, His will.[71]

It's God's will that His love touches and transforms hearts. It's His will that the oppressed find freedom. That the orphaned find a home. And when God has an agenda, He sends everyday people, like you and me, to bring it to completion.

God doesn't necessarily need to speak to us in a booming voice, commanding for us to act as the hands and feet of Jesus, when it is clearly written in Scripture. He has spoken to us through His Word, asking us to care for the orphaned. The needy. The poor and the hungry.

But the excuses we've created have served as obstacles, keeping us from taking that first step. These lies might whisper in our ears, "You're too young" or "You don't even have a high school diploma yet!" or "Do you *really* think you could make an impact with an issue this large?"

Just think about how much the Enemy loves it when we

make these excuses! Especially when we allow these lies to dictate our decisions. Isn't that his goal, after all? To thwart the kingdom of God from expanding? If the Enemy is hoping to expand his kingdom throughout the world and overtake God's throne (which obviously will never happen), it only makes sense he'd strive to block his opponents from expanding God's territory.

Therefore, it's *even more* crucial we become determined, bold as lions, and rise to carry out our God-given missions. We're on the winning team, after all, so why should we be afraid of failure?

I don't know what God has placed on your heart. Perhaps you've considered volunteering for a homeless shelter, sponsoring a child, or making an impact on your youth culture in some way. Whatever it is, that first step doesn't need to be drastic. No, we might not have the means to sponsor every child, but we can sponsor *one* child. It might be impossible to feed the mouths of every hungry person, but we can feed the mouth of *one* hungry person.

We may never know how much our small impact can grow from there.

Take Mordecai Ham, for example. Don't know who he is? This man is credited for being the first person to inspire the evangelist Billy Graham to become a pastor.[72] And we all know about the impact Billy Graham made, and continues to make, on the spread of Christianity throughout the world.

Just think—that spread began with a single flame lit on fire with God's love. God didn't ask Mordecai Ham to lead those *millions* of people to Christ. He only asked for him to take the first step in preaching the gospel. It was God's job to do the rest in multiplying Mordecai Ham's impact through Billy Graham.

So how can you take that first step in igniting your sphere of influence with God's light and love?

When Zach Hunter launched his campaign, Loose Change to Loosen Chains, to end slavery, he wasn't a celebrity figure. He didn't have the ability to bring millions of dollars into this campaign on his own. But he started where he could—in his own sphere of influence. The campaign was originally launched at his school, and then, of course, it snowballed from there.

Can you start with your own community? Is there a cause you feel compelled to take a stand for—such as the rights for the unborn or the need people have for clean water in Africa? And how can you use your voice, your unique influence as a teenager, to bring a necessary change to the youth culture around you?

Sure, the need you desire to meet might be great, but our God is greater. The only thing He asks of us is to take that first step. We are only responsible for igniting the single flame of love within us.

It's the Holy Spirit who can then take over, feeding that flame until it spreads into a wildfire of change.

Letter from Christ

I'm going to risk sounding old to you here, but when I was a small kid, snail mail was still the preferred method of writing to someone. Email was just beginning to take over the world, but it hadn't quite reached everyone yet. And social media certainly wasn't a thing.

Checking the mailbox every day was exciting for me. I couldn't wait to see if any of my friends wrote to me (even though they only lived a few miles down the road). Seeing my name inscribed onto the envelope made my heart beat a little quicker. That meant someone was thinking about me! They thought I was worthy enough to take the time to write me a letter.

Although we may not write snail mail letters as often as we did back then, we still serve as letters to everyone around us. Our words, our actions, and our lives speak a message.

What is the message you're speaking to your sphere of influence? Is it one that encourages others by showing them they are worthy and loved by God? That they are seen and chosen for a purpose?

The Bible itself uses this analogy of our lives serving as letters. Look at what Paul wrote in 2 Corinthians 3:2–3:

> *The only letter of recommendation we need is you yourselves. Your lives are a letter written in our hearts; everyone can read it and recognize our good work among you. Clearly, you are a letter from Christ showing the result of our ministry among you. This 'letter' is written not with pen and ink, but with the Spirit of the living God. It is carved not on tablets of stone, but on human hearts.*

Although Jesus is no longer on the earth in the flesh, He uses everyday flesh-and-blood people to carry His messages.

That's what this Scripture is talking about. But we must be willing to be used. We must open ourselves to the Spirit of God in our every interaction and encounter. Because a person may not read the Bible, but they are reading our life—and our life can be the letter that tells them about the gospel. That demonstrates Christ's redeeming power, displays His unconditional love, and proclaims victory for those in bondage and freedom for the oppressed.

And although your peers may have adults in their lives who know Jesus, your witness may potentially be more powerful. Why? Because you've grown up in the same generation as them. You understand the pressures of the current times—the relevant struggles—because you've experienced them firsthand. You're not merely a strict lifeguard who sits high in their stand on the shore, keeping a watchful eye on the swimmers, blowing a whistle any time things get out of hand. You're out there paddling in the harsh waters along with everyone else. And yet you've discovered the secret to staying afloat.

Your life and your love can be the evidence your peers need to place their trust in the Savior.

Will you be bold enough to make this kind of impact on your generation? God doesn't just use qualified adults with diplomas. In fact, later in 2 Corinthians 3, Paul writes, *"It is not that we think we are qualified to do anything on our own. Our qualification comes from God"* (v. 5).

Just think about that for a moment. *The Creator of the universe has qualified you, right now, to impact your sphere of influence.*

You may not be able to tell every teen in America about

Christ, but you can tell one person at a time. You can offer encouragement to the girl in the hallway who looks downhearted. You can serve as a listening ear to your friend. Sit with someone who looks lonely during lunch.

God has a lot to say to your generation about who He is and the salvation they can receive through His Son. I challenge you to be like a blank sheet of paper before Christ.

What is the message your peers are going to read through the life you live?

Chapter Eighteen
Striving to Impact, Not Impress

I have a love/hate relationship with Instagram. There are some positives to this social media platform I've grown to appreciate—such as the opportunity it provides to expand my readership, encourage others, and document my life. I also like the opportunities it provides to express my creativity and stay connected with others.

But I'll admit—this has become more of a *hate* relationship over the years. Why? Because I've noticed the effect it's had on our culture...especially us girls. It's only added to the pressure we feel to maintain a certain body type, wear trendy clothes, and create a persona we believe will garner more attention. And that's what we all crave, isn't it? Deep down, we only want to be accepted, approved of, and loved.

So we'll do everything we can to make that happen: Snap those cool photos of ourselves, get that new hair style, write some relevant and conversation-sparking captions, anything to keep those likes coming. To be the girl everyone wants to follow.

Even if it requires we only share the *filtered* version of ourselves.

Have you noticed this? It seems like Instagram is grooming us into becoming someone who yearns to impress rather than impact. It's teaching us to do everything we can to strive for acceptance and popularity—which is the opposite of what we have been called to do as followers of Christ.

The thing is, when our hearts have truly accepted our identity as a child of God, we no longer need to fight for the spotlight and applause. There's no amount of likes or followers that could grant us more than the love we already have in Christ. So instead of camouflaging ourselves to be like the world around us, we can develop new habits. Ones that aren't created for the purpose of swelling our egos or reducing our insecurities; rather, these habits can be used to further our God-given calling as an influencer.

Because the truth is, our quest for approval and attention is a natural part of being human—finding connection, fulfillment, and purpose. But what if I told you we could gain even deeper fulfillment through *impacting* instead of impressing? That our purpose will be uncovered not as we garner more likes, followers, and achievements, but as we go about directing more souls to the kingdom of God?

"Aren't You the Magic Man?"

In the 1960s and 70s, a middle-aged insurance salesman named George spent his weekends going door-to-door in several neighborhoods. But he wasn't selling insurance. Those who lived in these neighborhoods probably couldn't afford insurance anyway. These homes were located in an inner-city area of Georgia—areas known for their high crime rates. The families who lived here were among the poorest of the poor.

George wasn't hoping to gain something from these families, but to *give* to them instead. Not to sell but to entertain with magic tricks—specifically for the kids. Now, don't be alarmed: This wasn't *actual* magic he would perform. These were simple tricks anyone could learn, using only a coin. He would display a coin in his hand and reach out as if to give it to someone, but when he opened his hand, the coin had vanished.

And then he'd do the best part, the part the kids especially loved to witness. He'd reach out and retrieve the coin from behind someone's ear, pretending like it had been stuck inside their head.

These kids were in awe of these tricks and the man who performed them. They soon nicknamed this man "Magic Man."

But George didn't perform these tricks merely for their amusement.

You see, this was all part of his strategy for inviting these kids to attend the Sunday school he taught at the neighborhood clubhouse. Because once he captured their attention with those tricks, he had already won them over, so they were eager to attend. The parents often expressed concern that their kids didn't have nice clothes, but George always assured them they were welcome just as they were.

Over time—as the weeks grew into months, and the months grew into years—the news of Magic Man spread throughout the area. Kids from various nearby neighborhoods would gather to watch his tricks, and then they'd accept his invitation to attend Sunday school. Eventually, children weren't the only ones who came to hear his Bible teachings but also teens and adults. George would accept anyone who wanted to attend Sunday school, regardless of their age or economic status.

Fast forward about forty years. George was in his seventies, and although his Sunday school teaching years were over, he still lived in the same town in Georgia. One day, as he was at a supermarket shopping for groceries, he heard a voice behind him say, "Aren't you the magic man?"

It had been decades since George was last referred to by that nickname. He smiled and turned to face the lady. "I am."

Tears filled the woman's eyes. She went on to tell George her story—how she was one of the kids who had attended his Sunday school. It was the only church she'd ever been to. As she grew older and faced hardships of life, she would return to those days in Sunday school and sing the songs she'd learned in his class. Those song lyrics infused her with hope during tough times.

"I can't thank you enough for the impact you made on my life," the lady said, her eyes still brimming with tears.

This is only one of many stories George heard throughout the years about how his Sunday school impacted those kids. This influence never would've happened, of course, if he didn't first win them over with those simple coin tricks.

What I love about his story is George wasn't performing

these tricks merely for selfish attention and approval. That's not what compelled him to risk danger on the weekends by knocking on strangers' doors in the rough parts of town. It was his desire to spread the gospel that motivated him. The desire to leave an eternal impact.

Who was this magic man, you ask?

I am proud to say he was more than a "magic man" to me. He was none other than my granddaddy, George Biggar.

Jesus' Warning

What good would it have done for my granddaddy to do those magic tricks simply to entertain? He could've easily allowed the popularity to go to his head. To satisfy a thirst for human approval and recognition.

But he understood that our assignment as Christians is not to draw attention to ourselves. Sure, we may still gain favor with men as we pursue our gifts, but our purpose in drawing a crowd should never be so they can bow at our feet. The purpose should be so they can bow at the feet of our God instead.

Isn't this what Jesus did when He was on earth? Let's look at His life for a moment. Although His ministry started small among His twelve disciples, it soon spread as more people heard about His miracles. Pretty soon, large crowds gathered everywhere He went. Jesus worked tirelessly to meet the needs of lost and broken people, showing the Father's love by healing the sick and freeing the oppressed.

Yet never once did Jesus allow this popularity to go to

His head. The purpose in drawing the crowds wasn't to feed His pride but so He could feed their spiritual and physical needs.

That's the difference between impressing versus impacting.

And aren't we called to follow in the footsteps of Jesus Christ? We are called to be the "salt of the earth" (Matthew 5:13). We are here to "flavor" the world, to bless the world through our love.

This isn't possible unless we first understand our identity in Him. If we have not yet received the Father's love, if we do not ground our confidence in Him, then we will continue to slide back into old habits of seeking to please others and gain their approval. We will continue striving to gain more likes and followers to pacify our insecurities rather than trying to offer flavor to the world. And it will be impossible for us to carry out our calling while still trying to impress. Why? Because following our God-given assignment to impact often involves that we become rejected by others. Just like Jesus was.

So you can see why releasing our fear of people is a crucial step toward fulfilling our assignment. Jesus didn't call us to be friends with the world or gain favor with them, quite the opposite, actually! This is evident in James 4:4: *"You adulterers! Don't you realize that friendship with the world makes you an enemy of God? I say it again: If you want to be a friend of the world, you make yourself an enemy of God."*

Why do we make ourselves an enemy with God?

Because it is impossible to please both God and the world. It's that simple.

This explains the warning Jesus gave in Matthew 6:1–4:

Watch out! Don't do your good deeds publicly, to be admired by others, for you will lose the reward from your Father in heaven. When you give to someone in need, don't do as the hypocrites do—blowing trumpets in the synagogues and streets to call attention to their acts of charity! I tell you the truth, they have received all the reward they will ever get. But when you give to someone in need, don't let your left hand know what your right hand is doing. Give your gifts in private, and your Father, who sees everything, will reward you.

We cannot make an eternal impact if we are still searching for a pat on the back from others. This search for approval could cause us to "blow trumpets," as this passage says, so others can applaud us as we carry out our calling.

In other words, if we are still struggling with a desire to impress people, then our hearts won't be in the right place as we seek to further God's kingdom.

Isn't it interesting how Jesus addressed that warning? He exclaimed, "Watch out!" Typically, when we hear those words, our antennas shoot up. We were accustomed to hearing that caution several times a day as toddlers, back when we itched to touch a hot stove or play in the toilet bowl's water or cross the street. But it was for our own good that our parents yelled, "Watch out!" Just think about the many accidents they saved us from.

We didn't know it at the time though. That burning stove was begging for us to touch it! And what toddler *wouldn't* want to make a splash in a bowl of water sitting in the bathroom?

Yet our parents knew what was best for us. They could see

the danger that could result from giving in to those temptations, even if we were blind to them.

In the same way, when Jesus—God in flesh—proclaims to His children, "Watch out!" Don't you know it's for our best interest we heed His warning? He must see some disaster that could result if we were to follow our natural instinct to search for human approval and attention.

Actually, Jesus tells us what could happen if we *do* seek to impress: We would end up trading our eternal reward from God for a temporary reward of human approval.

Now, I don't know exactly what that eternal reward from God looks like, but I can assume an eternal, lasting reward from the Creator of the Universe is far richer than any temporary human applause. Wouldn't you think so too?

Garment of Love

Can you imagine how different the Bible would read if Jesus came to earth as an earthly prince or someone of high esteem? Instead of wearing a tunic made with only one piece of cloth, He would've worn a long robe to show off His high status. And rather than sandals that fell apart from frequent use, He'd have the means to wear a new pair of shoes each day. It's not like His Heavenly Father couldn't afford to provide for Him!

And yet, I believe Jesus chose this humble appearance on purpose. He didn't want to attract attention because of a high earthly status or striking attire; instead, He wanted people to be drawn to His outpouring of love. Rather than impressing with physical beauty, He chose to impact with eternal love. He must have wanted us to convey this kind of humble love as well. Look at what He says in Mark 12:38–40:

> *Jesus also taught: "Beware of these teachers of religious law! For they like to parade around in flowing robes and receive respectful greetings as they walk in the marketplaces. And how they love the seats of honor in the synagogues and the head table at banquets. Yet they shamelessly cheat widows out of their property and then pretend to be pious by making long prayers in public. Because of this, they will be more severely punished."*

Those teachers couldn't fool Jesus. He saw through their motives; He knew their intention was to impress rather than impact.

Now, let's not twist this to support the idea it's sinful to wear nice clothes. There's nothing wrong with wearing clothes that help us feel confident. Fashion is simply another way we can express ourselves! But don't you think it'd be freeing if we relented in our efforts of seeking attention? The race to keep up with the trends for the mere purpose of fitting in can get pretty exhausting at times.

What if we instead directed those efforts into pouring out God's love to those around us?

I love how Colossians 3:14 (MSG) describes the "outfit" we are called to wear as Christians: *"And regardless of what else you put on, wear love. It's your basic, all-purpose garment. Never be without it."*

Our world doesn't need another celebrity to worship. We don't need more people who, by showing off their beauty or achievements, leave others feeling less than and unworthy.

What we need is a generation who can capture the attention of men because of their garment of *love*. Young people whose speech is saturated with words of encouragement, whose eyes are attentive to those in need, whose hands are eager to reach out to help, and whose feet walk in the footsteps of Jesus.

If God is love, and He resides within us, then all that's required of us is to touch others with the same love that has touched us. And when they have become draped by this garment of love, then they, too, will be compelled to impact.

On and on this will go until Jesus' ministry has finally circled the globe.

Only then will the church, the bride of Christ, be *"like a bride beautifully dressed for her husband"* (Revelation 21:2)— glowing and radiant with God's love, fully prepared to reunite with her groom. The groom who is love Himself.

Jesus Christ.

Review

- There is no age requirement for God's kingdom; He can use people, young and old, to accomplish His purposes.

- God can use you now, in your sphere of influence— one person at a time—to make a difference.

- Instead of striving to impress others and gain popularity and approval in the eyes of others, let's strive to impact them with God's love. This is where our true purpose is found.

Replenish

"Don't let anyone think less of you because you are young. Be an example to all believers in what you say, in the way you live, in your love, your faith, and your purity" (1 Timothy 4:12).

"This is how we have discovered love's reality: Jesus sacrificed his life for us. Because of this great love, we should be willing to lay down our lives for one another. If anyone sees a fellow believer in need and has the means to help him, yet shows no pity and closes his heart against him, how is it even possible that God's love lives in him? Beloved children, our love can't be an abstract theory we only talk about, but a way of life demonstrated through our loving deeds. We know that the truth lives within us because we demonstrate love in action, which will reassure our hearts in his presence" (1 John 3:16–19, TPT).

"Here is how God's children can be clearly distinguished from the children of the Evil One. Anyone who does not demonstrate righteousness and show love to fellow believers is not living with God as his source. The beautiful message you've heard right from the start is that we should

walk in self-sacrificing love toward one another" (1 John 3:10-11, TPT).

"Those who are living in love are living in God, and God lives through them.... Our love for others is our grateful response to the love God first demonstrated to us" (1 John 4:16b, 19, TPT).

"For when we place our faith in Christ Jesus, there is no benefit in being circumcised or being uncircumcised. What is important is faith expressing itself in love" (Galatians 5:6).

Respond
Influencer Challenge

Use your sphere of influence on social media by sparking a discussion about this chapter with your friends! I challenge you to write a post that answers the following question. Be sure to use the hashtag #BecomeAnInfluencer in your response!

If you aren't on social media, no worries! You can participate in the same challenge among your friends in real life.

**What are simple ways you can express God's
love at school and in your everyday lives?**

Part Seven
Living the Influencer Lifestyle

Chapter Nineteen
Chosen For Now

I have always chosen to believe I am spiritually resilient. Someone who, with God's help, can face the storms of life, trusting a rainbow will magically appear on the other side. That's one of the many reasons I love writing fiction—because it reflects how, even though suffering is often necessary, it usually brings about those satisfying endings.

Cheesy, I know. But for those of us who are children of God, we can trust that all things can work together for our good (see Romans 8:28).

I thought this positive mindset was like a helmet, safeguarding my mind—until the blow of COVID hit, revealing this wasn't a helmet after all. *A flimsy hat* was more like it. At the beginning of the pandemic, I didn't have a problem with seeing through the lens of faith, but then those days turned into weeks. And, as you know, those weeks turned into months.

Now, I know being locked in the same place for so long factored into this decline, psychologically speaking. Regardless, it was like a dark cloud had settled over me. I felt void of the joy and peace in Christ that had once served as my anchor during life's storms.

I must not be the only one who questioned God's goodness and sovereignty during such chaos, fear, and confusion. Although I didn't lose a close family member during that time, I still felt a gaping hole in my heart. Why was God allowing nationwide division caused by the politics of the virus? Why were people so hateful in their violent protests? Were things ever going to return to normal?

Looking back, I failed to realize a certain truth: Evil is far more widespread than the virus will ever be. It will continue to infect people, even long after the pandemic has ended.

There is no escaping that reality. But there is also no escaping another more absolute reality:

The darkness that sweeps over this world can never be strong enough to blow out the light ablaze within us. And even though it looks like evil is winning, we know how the story ends. In the meantime, rather than watching as evil continues to infect more people, we have been given the cure this world is desperate for.

The cure of God's love. The cure of the gospel.

Are you hoping to see an end to this chaos and corruption as well? Great. Because God chose *you* to be born in this time of history for a reason. So that your spark of light can help to ignite a wildfire of God's love across the globe.

Truth is, we don't need to be defeated by evil. We are anointed by God to serve as an influencer for Him in today's culture. We can be empowered by the Holy Spirit to bring about the much-needed changes this world needs.

How can we go about doing this, and what might this require of us?

For Such a Time

There is one influencer in the Old Testament whose impact on the Jews continues to be celebrated today. She grew up in the country of Persia, and even though the year 479 BC sounds far removed from our world today, the culture was poisoned by the same type of malicious behavior that permeates ours as well.

And yet God had chosen Esther to be born in that time of history to make a unique impact. This impact wouldn't just make a difference in her culture but would be celebrated and remembered for generations to come.

As a kid, though, she may not have believed the plans God had in store for her. She was gifted with an outward beauty, but other than that, there wasn't anything extraordinary about her. She was an orphan and a Jew raised in a strange land by her cousin. Jews were not held in high regard at that time.

The book of Esther is long and intriguing, so I challenge you to read it for yourself to gather the entire story. But I'll give you the summarized version so you can see how God used this young woman in a special way—or, rather, how Esther came into agreement with how God wanted to use her.

It began one evening when King Ahasuerus (Xerxes) re-quested that Queen Vashti, his wife, show off her beauty before his friends while they were drunk. Not a fan of such an indecent and disrespectful request from her husband, she refused.

This infuriated the king. No doubt it kicked his pride a little.

As revenge, he banished the queen from his kingdom… but then he needed a new queen to take her place. So how did this king go about searching for this replacement? By holding a beauty contest.

This is where Esther steps into the story. When she was presented to the king, her striking beauty was difficult to miss—and of all the girls presented, Esther was chosen to become the next queen.

There was only one problem: The king didn't know Esther was a Jew. So when she was selected, her cousin Mordecai (the one who raised her) advised her to keep this little fact a secret.

The king had a right-hand man named Haman, and let's just say this man didn't have a problem with his self-confi-dence issue—if you know what I mean. In fact, he'd demand for people to bow to him. Ridiculous, right?

One Jewish man must have realized how absurd this was, because he refused to bow. This man, who happened to be Mordecai, angered Haman so much that he devised a plan to kill all the Jews. Including Mordecai. And when Mordecai found out about this, he was horrified! He con-fronted Esther and asked her to do him a favor. This wouldn't just be a favor for him but for all the Jews living in Persia at that time.

He asked Esther to approach the king, reveal her Jewish identity, and request for him to spare their lives.

At first, Mordecai's request no doubt terrified Esther. I don't blame her. After all, approaching the king without an invitation was against the law—even for the queen herself! Such an act could result in the death penalty.

As you can see, there was a lot at stake here. (Which is one reason why the story of Esther is so captivating!) Esther wasn't eager to fulfill this request by her cousin. As she hesitated, her cousin brought out this observation to her:

> *Mordecai sent this reply to Esther: "Don't think for a moment that because you're in the palace you will escape when all other Jews are killed. If you keep quiet at a time like this, deliverance and relief for the Jews will arise from some other place, but you and your relatives will die. Who knows if perhaps you were made queen for just such a time as this?"* (Esther 4:13–14).

I can imagine this comment causing Esther to do a little self-reflection. If I were in her shoes, I'd be arguing with myself back-and-forth—one part of myself would want to trust God, and the other side would be intimidated by the logistics of the situation. It seemed unlikely anyone would come out of this alive.

This hesitation is probably what led Esther to pray and fast.

She sent this response to her cousin: *"Go and gather together all the Jews of Susa and fast for me. Do not eat or drink for three days, night or day. My maids and I will do the same.*

And then, though it is against the law, I will go in to see the king. If I must die, I must die" (v. 16).

If I must die, I must die.

What a bold statement! She must have come to this realization: Even though the chances of making it out alive were slim, the chances of saving the Jews was worth the risk of her life. She must've known she was the only one who could potentially put an end to this plan. And maybe her cousin was right—perhaps she was placed in this position during that time for this very purpose.

So was it worth it? Did Esther succeed in her request to save the Jews?

Again, I'd like you to read the story of Esther yourself so you can see how it plays out. But I'll be happy to give you a spoiler alert.

Yes, she does succeed. The Jews are saved. Even Mordecai's life is spared.

The only person who is killed is Haman, the egotistical man who devised this evil plan to begin with.

It Begins With Us

Want to hear an interesting fact about the book of Esther? God's name isn't even mentioned once. And yet, in every twist and turn of the story, we see His hand at work. It looked like darkness was prevailing at times, and yet, when we step back, we see Him working behind the scenes from the very beginning of the story.

How many times does it appear as though God is

nowhere to be found in our society? I'm reminded of how I reacted to the pandemic during the lockdown. I questioned God's control because my mind was consumed with dwelling on the destruction.

And yet, God still has a plan for redemption. He hasn't forgotten about His children.

The story isn't over until it's over. And during the times when we are blind to His goodness and faithfulness, that's when we must draw closer to Him even more so. When our society is hard pressed with afflictions, that's when we can be used to help carry out God's ultimate plan of deliverance and redemption.

But we must be willing to be used *for such a time as this*—even, and *especially*, during such horrific conditions.

In 1 Peter 2:9, the Apostle Peter wrote that we are "a chosen people." The verse describes us as being "God's very own possession," and that we *can show others the goodness of God, for he called you out of the darkness into his wonderful light.*"

Why, then, should we remain in the mire of darkness when God is calling His possession into marvelous light?

In John 20:21, Jesus appeared to His disciples and breathed the Holy Spirit into them so they could be equipped to finish His ministry. He said to them, *"Peace be with you. As the Father has sent me, so I am sending you."*

The chaos of this world doesn't need to intimidate us with fear. The Holy Spirit emboldens and grants us peace so we, too, can finish Jesus' ministry. So we can carry out our influencer duties in bringing hope in the midst of pain, peace in the midst of a storm, and light in the midst of darkness. It is

God's desire, His plan, for people to be rescued and restored and delivered from destruction.

But this plan needs to be set into motion by both prayer and our individual acts of faith.

Perhaps we have been chosen for this very moment in history. So we can make an impact that only we can make with our lives. And perhaps the change we hope to see in this world begins with us taking that bold leap of faith.

That change begins with us.

Chapter Twenty
Are We Willing to Bear His Name?

G rowing up in a free country—one that exercises the freedom of speech and religion—I've never had to worry much about persecution. Not like the Christians in other countries and time periods have, at least. I'll admit this is a freedom I've often taken for granted.

Because now, I'm starting to witness persecution against Christians weaving itself into our society in subtle manners. The "cancel culture" of our world chooses to shun, reject, humiliate, threaten, and silence those whose beliefs do not align with theirs. Those who may have made a statement, or performed an action, that goes against the ideological standards society has created. These standards often completely violate the standards of ultimate truth found in God's Word.

Cancel culture is like hanging up the phone on someone because you don't agree with them—and then doing everything you can do to make that person's life miserable.

It's the very definition of immaturity in my opinion.

And if you haven't noticed, our biblical values are not popular in the world's eyes. These "old-fashioned principles," as the world often describes them, have been twisted to appear unloving in a world where anything goes and there is no absolute truth.

In an effort to appease society, are we going to go with the flow and bow down to the culture—even if it requires watering down God's Word?

Because the thing is, as an influencer for Christ, we can't escape persecution. The Enemy's goal is to thwart the kingdom of God from advancing. His tactics involve pressuring us Christians with threats of humiliation. Shame. Rejection. Ridicule. This is the very type of persecution Jesus faced when He carried His cross. It's as though the Enemy is whispering in our ears, "You don't need to bear your cross anymore. It's not going to hurt for you to put it down and take a break. After all, if you keep carrying it, there's a mob of people who are prepared to slander your name in the dirt. Do you really want to ruin your life and your reputation?"

You see, there's a reason why Christianity—and the name of Jesus—has been controversial for centuries. Because the spirit of the world is intimidated by us. He's intimidated by the power we possess, through the Holy Spirit, as we carry out our influencer duties.

Therefore, we must be *even more determined* not to bow to the pressures of society. The pressures that tempt us to forsake the standards of God's Word.

And we must do as Jesus commanded us to *"give up your own way, take up your cross, and follow me"* (Matthew 16:24).

Even if we risk being the next cancel culture victim.

So when the time comes for us to stand up for the truth and represent Christ in the midst of our perverse culture, we will be presented with a choice: Will we cave under society's idolization of approval and acceptance? Or will we choose to be dictated by our inner convictions instead and represent Jesus well despite the costs?

Culture Warriors

If your family has ever moved to a new town or across states, or even across the world, then perhaps you're familiar with the scary feeling of embracing unfamiliar territory. Although my family never made a big move when I was a kid, I can recall visiting New York City for the first time as a teen and how dizzy I felt with culture shock. (Or maybe those were simply claustrophobia symptoms caused by lack of space!)

There are four young men in the Old Testament who undoubtedly experienced a major culture shock back in their day as well. Daniel, Shadrach, Meshach, and Abednego were among the Jews deported from their home of Judah and sent to live in the strange land of Babylon—a land that did not keep God at the forefront of their culture. Not only that, but these young men had been recruited to serve in the royal palace. This required them to go through a three-year training regiment, a reprogramming, that would mold these Jews to give up their former ways and blend in with their new Babylonian culture.

During this training, they were even pressured to eat like

the Babylonians—but they believed doing so would violate God's food laws in the Torah.

These young men could have easily caved into the pressure. I'm sure it seemed harmless to take a bite out of the king's meat, just like everyone else was doing. But rather than giving in for the sake of blending in, they instead stood strong in their convictions. Daniel 1:8 says that Daniel *"was determined not to defile himself by eating the food and wine given to them by the king."*

That was only the beginning of their testing.

If you've been in the church for a while, you may already know the story of how God rescued Shadrach, Meshach, and Abednego from being destroyed in a fiery furnace. But I doubt the story played out exactly like the VeggieTales® version! (For one, they were *human* rather than vegetables. As far as I know.) These young men were among those commanded to bow to a golden statue that King Nebuchadnezzar had set up to represent him and his power.

Shadrach, Meshach, and Abednego knew the punishment in store for those who refused to bow. So can you imagine how terrified they must have been? No doubt, their legs trembled in fear as they stood rather than knelt. How tempting it must have been for them to tell God, "I'm going to bow, but you see my heart, don't you? This really doesn't mean anything."

But their actions—their demonstration of loyalty to God—spoke far louder than their words.

The king even gave these men one more chance to bow. Yet they remained unwavering in their bold stance toward God. As a result, they were thrown into the blazing furnace—a furnace heated seven times hotter than usual! So hot, in fact, the flames killed the soldiers who threw them inside.

But the saving power of their God was greater than the destructive power of those flames. Not only was God with them in the fire, but He was able to deliver them from the furnace without even a small burn.

I bet they gave the biggest sigh of relief as they stepped out of there!

Guess what resulted because of their faithfulness? When it became obvious that God had saved them, King Nebuchadnezzar gave glory to God and promoted these men to a higher office in Babylon.

In other words, their witness was strengthened.

Daniel was presented with a similar opportunity to demonstrate his loyalty to God. There were high officers and administrators who must have been jealous of the favor given to him by the king because they devised a plan against him and convinced the king to pass a decree. This law stated, if anyone were to pray for the following thirty days to anyone other than King Darius, that person must be thrown into the lions's den.

But Daniel stood as a warrior for the Lord, committed to God's law rather than man's law. So, he was thrown into the lion's den, but God was with Him in there just like he had been with his friends, Shadrach, Meshach, and Abednego. God kept the mouths of the lions shut, and they were unable to destroy him.

When the king noticed God had rescued him, Daniel's witness became strengthened as well. Daniel 6:25–26a says, *"Then King Darius sent this message to the people of every race* and nation and language throughout the world: 'Peace and prosperity to you! I decree that everyone throughout my kingdom should tremble with fear before the God of Daniel.'"

Daniel, like his friends, chose to be a warrior for God and, as a result, God's fame spread throughout Babylon and led to the saving of that nation.

Compromise or Confront?

Raise your hand if you can proudly proclaim that you like to be seen as different.

Anybody?

Now, maybe there are some of you who did raise your hands. But for those of us who have that human tendency to desire approval and acceptance, we kept our hands safely in our laps, *thankyouverymuch*. From the moment we were born, we've been conditioned to blend in with the world around us.

In today's society, it's cool to be like everyone else. I get it. But this can become an issue if it holds us back from being an influencer for Christ.

Let's have an honest heart-to-heart for a moment: If you were given an opportunity like the one Daniel and his three friends had, would your desire for approval tempt you to go with the flow?

My automatic response to that question is, "Of course not!" But how many times have I failed to represent Christ in public? When have I allowed my fear of human opinion to water down my witness for Jesus?

You see, an influencer for Christ doesn't just take a stand when the consequences are deadly. An influencer for Christ takes a stand even in the small opportunities of our everyday lives—times when we can choose to either be dictated by biblical values or by worldly values.

Times when we can choose to either *compromise* or *confront*.

Why is it often harder for us to represent Christ in these small daily opportunities? Perhaps because we think lowering our standards in a "small way" may not truly make a difference.

But it's in these times, when there doesn't seem to be much at stake, that our heart for God and His Word shine through. Our adoration for Him isn't just displayed when we refuse to bow to a statue; it's displayed when we refuse to join with other girls in making fun of a classmate's outlandish choice of style. Our love for Christ isn't just demonstrated when we stand up for Him publicly but also when we share our faith with others at school.

If everyone else around us is going with the flow—caving beneath the pressures of our culture—then how long until Christianity is washed away from the core of our society altogether? If we as Christians choose to blend with the world, then who is going to be the one to pass the gospel down to the next generation?

Speaking out about biblical truths can be intimidating...especially when no one else is doing it. But the silence shouldn't excuse us from raising our voices and speaking truth.

It should prompt us to speak up even louder.

Why do you think King Nebuchadnezzar tried to indoctrinate Daniel and his three friends with the Babylonian worldly lifestyles and worldviews? Because he wanted to expand his own kingdom, right? He wanted them to adapt values that were in opposition to God's Law.

The way in which our modern world attempts to indoctrinate us is often more subtle. We must take heed of the warning found in Ephesians 6:11–12:

Put on all of God's armor so that you will be able to stand firm against all strategies of the devil. For we are not fighting against flesh-and-blood enemies, but against evil rulers and authorities of the unseen world, against mighty powers in this dark world, and against evil spirits in the heavenly places.

Why must we put on this armor? So we will have the courage to confront rather than compromise. So we will remain standing when everyone else is kneeling to the idols of this world. The purpose is not merely to come across as a culture rebel but rather to spark a culture *revival.*

That is exactly what Daniel and the other three (because their names are too long to type out) did in their bold stance for God.

It looked like they were headed into defeat, right? I mean, what could be more deadly than a fiery furnace and a lion's den? But they knew a truth the Babylonians failed to see:

Victory wasn't going to arrive only if God saved them from death.

Victory had already been won the moment they risked everything to take a stand for Him.

Avoiding the Greatest Regret

Remember when Peter denied Christ, attempting to escape persecution? Not just once. Not just twice. But *three times* he claimed that he didn't know Jesus. And after all Jesus had done for him!

When Peter realized his mistake, what was his reaction? Luke 22:62 tells us that, *"Peter left the courtyard, weeping bitterly."*

Why did he weep? Because he knew just how great of an offense his denial was toward the One who had changed and saved his life.

Jesus bore our sin and suffering on the cross, so the least we can do is bear His name on this earth.

Even if it makes us unpopular. Even if it requires rejection. Humiliation. Which, most likely, it will. Because if you haven't noticed yet, the name Jesus is probably the most simultaneously *loved* and *hated* name in the world. It always has been, and it always will be until He returns. That's what Jesus meant when He said to the disciples, in John 15:18–19, *"If the world hates you, remember that it hated me first. The world would love you as one of its own if you belonged to it, but you are no longer part of the world. I chose you to come out of the world, so it hates you."*

Doesn't sound like much of a motivational pep talk if you ask me!

But even though the Enemy thought he was winning when the Romans persecuted Jesus on the cross—spitting and laughing in His face—we know how the rest of the story went down.

That persecution wasn't strong enough to hold back the power of God.

During those times when it looks like the Enemy is winning as we face persecution in this world, we know that isn't the case. Because he's quite dumb, if you ask me. He keeps forgetting the plot twist. And that is this:

Despite his best efforts, he was unable to hold Jesus down; in fact, those attempts only served to *strengthen* Jesus' ministry instead of *thwarting* it.

So when we face rejection and ridicule because of the Name we carry, let's consider it to be ammunition for our role as influencer.

On Judgment Day, as we stand face-to-face before the King, we will not regret the ways we expressed our devotion to Him on this earth. The approval of men is temporary. But the approval of God? And the impact we could make on the souls around us because of our witness?

That, my friend, will last forever.

Chapter Twenty-One
Making Him Famous

*O*ut of curiosity, I did a quick Google search to discover ways to become famous. I didn't even need to type the entire inquiry, either, because apparently that question has already been searched by thousands of others. Here are some of the suggestions that popped onto my screen:

Audition for a reality show. (Until someone comes up with a way to present a competition show for writers, then that'll need to be scratched from my list. There's no way I'm meeting my future husband on a dating reality show!)[73]

Set a Guinness world record. (I currently type 128 words per minute. With determination and practice, what if I could set a record?)[74]

Film yourself doing something crazy and stupid to attract viral online attention. (That just doesn't sit well with this introvert.)[75]

Build your social media platform. (I've already tried doing that, but it's not as easy as it sounds!)[76]

Well, according to the ever-so-trusty Google, it looks like there's not much hope for me to make my mark in Fame Land. Or maybe there could be if I truly tried hard enough to make my name greater. If I devoted every hour of my day into building my fame, popularity, and credentials, would I someday see my name in flashing lights? Would people soon plaster posters of my face onto their bedroom walls or create fan page accounts for me on social media?

Maybe one day, with a swollen ego, I'll be able to kick back and give a big sigh of relief and proclaim, "Finally. People admire me. I made it."

Only...I don't think it would work that way. Because I don't think admiration of others could ever grant me satisfaction nor fulfillment.

It seems like it could, though, doesn't it? For centuries, we've looked up to celebrities. We've named hairstyles after them. Purchased the same dress they wore to a party. Patterned our eyeliner after theirs. No wonder the search inquiry "how can I become famous" is so...well, popular! Because fame sounds like it'd grant everything we could possibly desire, doesn't it?

But just ask any celebrity out there, and if they're truthful, they will share that being famous is not all it appears to be.

We were never created to spread our own fame. The swollen egos it produces often leads to destruction in the end. Perhaps this is the "death" that Proverbs 14:12 (NIV) refers to: *"There is a way that appears to be right, but in the end it leads to death."*

So what if we devoted our energies into spreading *Jesus'* name rather than our own?

You may say, "Yeah, but He's already famous." True. But did you know there are thirty million people who will die in this year alone who have never heard the name of Christ?[77]

Matthew 24:14 tells us Jesus isn't going to return until *every nation* has had the chance to hear the good news of the gospel.

The thing is, we don't need another name in lights. We don't need another celebrity to worship. What we need— what God is looking for—are people who can be devoted to spreading His name rather than their own. People who are willing to dedicate their lives not just in following Him, but in reaching the unreached. Telling the hopeless there is hope. Saving souls from eternal destruction. Fame could never grant us a greater honor than the honor we have as an influencer for Christ.

What does it look like to carry this good news throughout the earth, and how can we begin?

Can't Help BUt Share

Have you ever been so enthusiastic about your experience with a product that you couldn't help but tell your friends? This is basically what a brand influencer does on Instagram, YouTube, and TikTok. I've seen influencers who have raved about a certain shampoo's hair-growth-producing power. They nearly won me over with their contagious enthusiasm as they showed off the results by displaying their before-and-after pictures. (I say *nearly* because the price tag was far too high for me to consider!)

Brands understand the power of a testimony and the potential it brings to generate new sales. It's why they hire influencers to rave about their products online. That's called word-of-mouth marketing.

Now, think about the people in the Bible who could be considered influencers for Christ. These are the people who, with enthusiasm, contributed to the spreading of Jesus' fame early in His ministry. There were several of them—Paul. Peter. John.

The very first person who is credited to telling others about Jesus' transformative ways, however, was not a disciple. This person wasn't even a man. Or reputable, for that matter.

She was an outcast in society. Her name isn't mentioned in the Bible, but she is known as "the Samaritan woman" or the "woman at the well."

Jesus first meets this woman on his journey through Samaria as He travels to Galilee. He had stopped along the journey to rest at a well, and it is there that He meets this woman.

But it's odd that Jesus would encounter a woman at the well at this time of day. Why?

First, women typically drew from the well in groups. It was a social hangout of sorts. And yet this Samaritan woman was alone.

Second, this was the hottest part of the day. Probably around noon. Most people would try to avoid the heat by drawing from the well in the early morning or later in the evening.

So was this woman intentionally trying to avoid the other women in her town? It's easy to believe she was looked down on by them because of the choices she'd made. She had been married to five different husbands, and she was living with her boyfriend at the time of her meeting with Jesus.

Her choices caused her to be despised by the people in her village, but it wasn't enough to prevent Jesus from talking with her. He approaches and asks for a drink, and she responds with a question of her own: *"Why are you asking me for a drink?"* (John 4:9).

She probably asked this because most women were disregarded by men at that time. Not to mention, Jesus was a Jew, and Jews didn't associate with Samaritans.

His response was not what she had probably expected: *"If you only knew the gift God has for you and who you are speaking to, you would ask me, and I would give you living water"* (v. 10).

Obviously, Jesus was only trying to spark a conversation with this woman—not one about physical water, but one about *eternal* water. He knew this woman was dehydrated spiritually and that her thirst could only be quenched with His eternal life and love.

He then says to her, *"Anyone who drinks this water will soon become thirsty again. But those who drink the water I give will never be thirsty again. It becomes a fresh, bubbling spring within them, giving them eternal life"* (vv. 13–14).

The Samaritan woman understood Jesus was speaking in figurative language. See if you can sense the desperation in her response: *"'Please, sir,' the woman said, 'give me this water! Then I'll never be thirsty again, and I won't have to come here to get water'"* (v. 15).

Jesus then surprises this woman by telling her He knows about her shady history with men. He doesn't say this from a place of condemnation or accusation—even though I'm sure she was convicted about these matters. But rather than being ashamed, she's astonished because she recognizes Jesus is not just any human. She first assumes He's a prophet, but then He says to her, "I am the Messiah!" (v. 26).

That's all she needed to hear. Her quench for *more* had finally been satisfied.

This woman became so excited to have met the Messiah that she dropped her water jar. Physical water could never satisfy the way this new eternal water did! She took off in a rush—not out of fear. Not out of shame. But out of *excitement*. This eternal water was gushing from her heart, bubbling over with joy from the love she had encountered with this man.

And she couldn't help but share this good news. No longer did she consider the typical contempt the townspeople held toward her. She disregarded their opinion as she, in enthusiasm, said to them, *"Come and see a man who told me everything I ever did! Could he possibly be the Messiah?"* (v. 29).

Finishing His Work

Isn't it interesting how the Samaritan woman now ran toward the very people she usually tried to run *away* from? What she had to share became more important than their opinion of her, and this new living water infused her with invigoration, boldness, purpose, and joy.

Now, I can't help but ask . . .

Have we allowed the good news of Jesus Christ to fuel us into sharing our testimony as well?

Are we overflowing with Christ's eternal water so much that we can't help but spill it into the lives of others?

Let's think about those Instagram influencers again. They're not trying to sell the product to current customers, are they? Of course not! They're hoping to show the non-customers what they could miss out on if they don't give this awesome hair-growth-inducing shampoo a try.

That perspective helps us understand this Scripture:

For "Everyone who calls on the name of the Lord will be saved." But how can they call on him to save them unless they believe in him? And how can they believe in him if they have never heard about him? And how can they hear about him unless someone tells them? (Romans 10:13–14).

You may say, "Yeah, but pretty much everyone in this nation knows about Christianity." That may be true—especially in the Bible belt where I grew up. There's practically a church on every corner!

So, yes, the people you encounter today might already know about Christianity. But do they know about *Jesus?*

Have they heard about the life-transforming eternal water He offers? Or are they only familiar with church buildings and cross necklaces and hymns they hear at funerals?

If social media influencers sold products the way some of us Christians "sell" Christianity, I doubt they'd make much of a profit. They don't just make a video of themselves holding the container and saying, "This shampoo bottle would look beautiful sitting inside of your shower."

Why? Because people aren't going to pay fifty dollars on shampoo simply because of how a container looks.

Influencers understand that principle. They need to share *the results* a product offers—that luxurious hair you've been wanting. The feeling of confidence you'll have as you witness new hair growth.

To do this, they discuss their own experience with it… their hair transformation. That's why you may see those before-and-after pictures on these types of posts!

Isn't this the kind of approach the Samaritan woman used when she said, *"Come and see a man who told me everything I ever did!"* (John 4:29).

I doubt she would've had that much enthusiasm, however, if Jesus had spoken with her from a place of condemnation. Imagine what would've happened if He said something like, "What you're doing is wrong. You need to repent of your sins. God doesn't approve of that adulterous kind of lifestyle. I would know—I am His Son, after all."

That wouldn't have won her heart over to Him! Yes, Jesus *did* confront this woman of her sins, but this came from a place of love, mercy, and compassion rather than judgment.

The unbelievers around us—those living a sinful lifestyle—aren't going to be sold on Jesus if they only receive condemnation from us. Instead, they need to be told that, despite whatever their lifestyle is and past may be, Jesus has come to rescue them. That His cleansing grace is powerful enough to wash away their yesterdays.

Because it's not condemnation and judgment that they're thirsty for.

It's the eternal water that can only be provided by Jesus Christ. The love that can overflow from us and spill into their lives, prompting the much-needed change within their hearts and lives.

When the Samaritan woman left Jesus, as we read about in John 4, the disciples then came to Jesus and urged Him to eat something. He responded by saying, *"I have a kind of food you know nothing about"* (v. 32). He then said that His food, His true sustenance, comes from *"doing the will of God, who sent me, and from finishing his work"* (v. 34).

Spreading God's kingdom was the nourishment that kept Jesus moving forward.

And it can be ours as well. Because as children of God, we, too, have been called to finish His work despite our past. Despite our failures and weaknesses and social status and follower count on social media. Because just like with the Samaritan woman, there isn't an application to fill out when it comes to advancing the gospel. We have already been chosen and accepted as influencers.

It began the very moment we received Jesus Christ as our Savior.

It's Harvest Time!

If you've come this far in the book, I hope by now you believe the truth that you do have potential as an influencer. I hope you're encouraged to close this book (once you finish it, of course) and get to work sharpening your gifts for the kingdom.

But there's some of you who are still on the fence. Some

of you who are still doubting your influencing abilities, as though it comes from *yourself* rather than from Christ within you.

How do I know this?

Because I used to be the same way. No, not *used to*— because there are still times, even today, when I have self-doubts. Times when I'm tempted to make excuses like, "Atheists are already steadfast in their beliefs that God doesn't exist. Who am I to think I can change their minds?"

And then God reminds me: I'm not called to change their minds. We receive Jesus by *faith*, not by intellect. The truth is, God has already prepared the people around us to hear the Good News. Yes, even the atheists. It may look as though their minds are made up; however, we know this truth:

Everyone who has not received Jesus is spiritually dehydrated. Their hearts are ready to receive this eternal water.

After Jesus met with the Samaritan woman, He gave this challenge to His disciples: *"But I say, wake up and look around. The fields are already ripe for harvest"* (John 4:35).

Notice the language Jesus used there: *Wake up and look around.* He's calling each of us to remain alert and attentive to those around us—the needs people have to receive the Truth.

Their hearts are "ripe for harvest," as that verse says. In the Bible, *harvest* is used as an analogy of souls won for God's kingdom. We have been called to be harvesters. (As I mentioned before, my name literally means *harvester*, but I don't want to be alone in doing this!) We can share the Good News with them. We can show them the transformation that has taken place within our lives in a "before-and-after" Christ.

We might not see immediate results after one conversation, but that's okay. It takes time for a seed that's planted deep into the soil to take root and grow into a sprout. The same is with a seed planted within the heart. It takes time to become manifested.

In the verses that follow in John 4, Jesus built on this harvest analogy: *"The harvesters are paid good wages, and the fruit they harvest is people brought to eternal life. What joy awaits both the planter and the harvester alike!"* (v. 36).

There is *joy* in furthering God's kingdom! Not just here on earth, but in eternity, too, when we reap our "good wages."

Jesus is waiting for each of us to do our part in making His name famous—because it's only then, when the entire world knows His name, that He will come again (see Matthew 24:14).

Up until this point, there haven't been enough people willing to devote their lives to the spreading of His fame. This is what Jesus meant when He told the disciples, *"The harvest is great, but the workers are few"* (Matthew 9:37).

I pray we will accept our invitation to work in the fields of harvest.

That we will develop an eyesight to see the spiritual needs of those around us.

That we will remain passionate, just like Jesus was, to finish His Father's work.

That we will find our purpose in surrendering our life to God.

That we will *"be a special utensil for honorable use"* and

"ready for the Master to use you for every good work" (2 Timothy 2:21)—so that we can impact this generation for Christ.

And I pray we will continue this ministry with boldness, empowered by the same supernatural confidence that the disciples were: *"But you will receive power when the Holy Spirit comes upon you. And you will be my witnesses, telling people about me everywhere—in Jerusalem, throughout Judea, in Samaria, and to the ends of the earth"* (Acts 1:8).

The harvest fields are ripe and ready. Souls are waiting for your influence. No, you might not be able to reach them all. But if each of us do our own part in collecting the harvest, then soon, the entire world will someday know the name of the Lord Jesus Christ (see Philippians 2:10–11).

First things first. It's time to roll up your sleeves and get started.

Your work as an influencer has only just begun.

Review

- We have been chosen for this day in history to make a unique influence on our culture for Christ—despite the costs.

- As Christians, we will face persecution, rejection, and humiliation. This is part of the "cross" we bear. Will we be ready when the time comes? Are we willing to bear His name among our perverse culture?

- We are called to prepare this world for Jesus' second coming. This can only happen when we each do our part in making Jesus famous. There is no greater honor than this!

Replenish

"But it is no shame to suffer for being a Christian. Praise God for the privilege of being called by his name!" (1 Peter 4:16).

"For I am not ashamed of this Good News about Christ. It is the power of God at work, saving everyone who believes— the Jew first and also the Gentile" (Romans 1:16).

"Therefore, go and make disciples of all the nations, baptizing them in the name of the Father and the Son and the Holy Spirit. Teach these new disciples to obey all the commands I have given you. And be sure of this: I am with you always, even to the end of the age" (Matthew 28:19–20).

"For 'Everyone who calls on the name of the Lord will be saved.' But how can they call on him to save them unless they believe in him? And how can they believe in him if they have never heard about him? And how can they hear about him unless someone tells them?" (Romans 10:13–14).

"Then I heard the Lord asking, 'Whom should I send as a messenger to this people? Who will go for us?' I said, 'Here I am. Send me' (Isaiah 6:8).

Respond
Influencer Challenge

Use your sphere of influence on social media by sparking a discussion about this chapter with your friends! I challenge you to write a post that answers the following question. Be sure to use the hashtag #BecomeAnInfluencer in your response!

If you aren't on social media, no worries! You can participate in the same challenge among your friends in real life.

What does it look like to be an influencer for Jesus in today's culture? What are some of the costs, requirements, and rewards for living the influencer lifestyle?

Accepting Jesus as Your Personal Savior

How can you accept Jesus Christ as your personal Savior, and what does this mean?

First, you must believe we can only attain salvation through God's Son, Jesus Christ. There is no other way to the Father or to eternal life than through Him (see John 14:6, Acts 4:12, and 1 Timothy 2:5).

Why did God send His Son to redeem His children? Because it was impossible to attain true, eternal salvation elsewhere. You see, God wanted to rescue us from the condemnation of our sins. When Adam and Eve sinned in the Garden of Eden, their sin separated mankind from God and banished us from His presence. God is a holy God, and sin cannot enter His presence—unless, however, there is an outpouring of blood, because blood contains life, and this life purifies, cleanses, and purges the death of sin. Before Jesus died, animal sacrifices had to be made to enter God's holy presence and receive pardon for their sins.

But this was never God's original plan. His heart is to have an intimate relationship with His children, and He longs for us to spend all of eternity with Him. Besides, animal sacrifices were never powerful enough. It was only Jesus' pure and holy blood that could grant mankind total remission from our sins. John 3:16 says, *"For this is how God loved the world: He gave his one and only Son, so that everyone who believes in him will not perish but have eternal life."* Jesus Christ laid down His life as a blood offering on our behalf—because it was only His pure, undefiled, and life-giving blood that could forever banish death's stronghold. On that cross Jesus received the torture, humiliation, and rejection that would have otherwise been reserved for us.

But the sin of this world could not keep Him down. A few days later, Jesus rose from the dead. When Jesus died, our sins and former life were buried, but when He rose, our new life rose as well (see 2 Corinthians 5:17 and Romans 6:4). We are now free to be the new creation He has called us to be. We are free to live the abundant life He purchased for us rather than remaining in the bondage of death (caused by sin). And best of all, we now have direct access to God's holy presence at any time of the day. We are now in right standing with the Father once again—and we don't even need to make animal sacrifices! Those of us who believe in Jesus as our Savior can look forward to an entire eternity of living in God's presence. John 5:24 says, *"They will never be condemned for their sins, but they have already passed from death into life."*

Do you want this new life God is offering you? Are you

ready to accept the gift Jesus purchased by the outpouring of His blood?

This invitation is open to *everyone*—regardless of your background, race, reputation, or former religion. Jesus didn't die just for the Bible belt in America. He didn't die for the "good"; He died for the broken. That includes *all of us*. Jesus *"wants everyone to be saved and to understand the truth"* (1 Timothy 2:4). 1 John 2:2 says, *"He himself is the sacrifice that atones for our sins—and not only our sins but the sins of all the world."*

So if you're ready to accept this invitation, here's all you need to do. (It's really not complicated!)

1. Believe that Jesus Christ is the only way to receive salvation, access God the Father, and receive redemption from our sins.

2. Admit your need for a Savior who can rescue you from the destruction and stronghold of death (caused by sin).

3. Believe that Jesus Christ died and rose from the grave on your behalf so you can be redeemed and live a new life, one that is devoted to Him.

4. Ask Jesus Christ to come into your heart through the Holy Spirit and become your Lord and Savior. Surrender your life to Him and His purposes. Romans 10:9 says, *"If you openly declare that Jesus is Lord and believe in your heart that God raised him from the dead, you will be saved."*

Sample Prayer

Dear God, thank You for sending Your Son to die on the cross for my sins. I am so grateful that Jesus bore the suffering on my behalf so I could live a life of freedom. Jesus, I admit my shortcomings and my need for a Savior. Could You forgive me for all my sins? I don't want to live apart from You anymore and miss out on this relationship. I believe You gave Your life for me so I could live totally surrendered to You. And now, I invite You, through the power of the Holy Spirit, to come into my heart and become my Lord and Savior. I want to do life *for* You and *with* You from now on. Help me to grow in You daily and to become an influencer for Your kingdom. It's in Your name I pray. Amen.

> *"And this is what God has testified: He has given us eternal life, and this life is in his Son. Whoever has the Son has life; whoever does not have God's Son does not have life"* (1 John 5:11–12).

> *"Jesus spoke to the people once more and said, "I am the light of the world. If you follow me, you won't have to walk in darkness, because you will have the light that leads to life"* (John 8:12).

> *"All who declare that Jesus is the Son of God have God living in them, and they live in God. We know how much God loves us, and we have put our trust in his love. God is love, and all who live in love live in God, and God lives in them"* (1 John 4:15–16).

"And since we have been made right in God's sight by the blood of Christ, he will certainly save us from God's condemnation. For since our friendship with God was restored by the death of his Son while we were still his enemies, we will certainly be saved through the life of his Son. So now we can rejoice in our wonderful new relationship with God because our Lord Jesus Christ has made us friends of God" (Romans 5:9–11).

Acknowledgments

The idea and outline of this book took shape during a personal writing retreat right before the pandemic hit in March 2020. Little did I know just how desperate our world would soon become for the light, peace, and hope we carry!

My mom joined me in that retreat to the Blue Ridge Mountains and served as a listening ear as I shared this idea with her. Her encouragement gave me the nudge I needed to move forward with developing it into a book. For that reason, I want to begin by acknowledging her and the countless hours she has devoted to supporting my writing journey over the years.

I give credit to *both* of my parents for every book I write. Their faith and belief have given me the freedom to pursue my writing dreams since I was a teenager. They have also shown me, by example, what it looks like to focus on *eternal* pursuits—loving God and loving others. So if you, reader, were inspired in this book to spend your teen years wisely, then thank my parents for the impact they left on me!

I am also beyond blessed to have sisters, cousins, aunts,

and grandmas who see and understand my heart to write books as a ministry. Thank you for the prayers, the encouraging text messages, and the many ways you have supported this journey. Your godly influence on my life has shaped me into who I am today.

I also want to acknowledge everyone else who has left their fingerprints on this project in some way...

Cyle Young, for connecting this project with the perfect publishing home.

Victoria Duerstock, for believing in this book and breathing life into so many dreams at End Games Press.

To my editors, Hope Bolinger and Nikki Wright, for your attention to detail and for catching those typos and embarrassing content inconsistencies.

And to every reader who has expressed your support in my writing career over the years—by posting book reviews, sending an email, tagging me on social media, or sharing books with friends. It has always been my prayer that you will close these books with a greater desire and determination to chase after God and experience the fullness of His love. I can't wait to hear about how He uses you and your unique gifts for the advancement of His kingdom!

Last but most important, thank you to my Heavenly Father for the opportunity to influence this generation to be an influencer for You. May You receive all the glory, honor, and praise through each and every book I write.

About the Author

Tessa Emily Hall is an award-winning author who wrote her debut novel, *Purple Moon,* when she was sixteen. She is now a multi-published author and speaker who encourages teens to embrace their unique potential and gifts to further God's kingdom. Her articles can be found in multiple publications, including Crosswalk. com, *Devozine, Guide Magazine, Broken But Priceless Magazine,* Fervr.net, and more. When Tessa's fingers aren't flying 128 WPM across the keyboard, she can be found sipping on a latte, teaching at writing conferences across the country, creating art journals, and acting in inspirational films. Her favorite way to procrastinate is to connect with readers on her mailing list, social media (@tessaemilyhall), and website: www.tessaemilyhall.com.

Endnotes

1   "'Fireproof' Actor Kirk Cameron Shares Testimony at
    Baptist College – Baptist News Global." Last modified
    November 23, 2010.

2   "'Fireproof' Actor Kirk Cameron Shares Testimony at Baptist
    College – Baptist News Global." Baptist News Global, Last
    modified November 23, 2010. https://baptistnews.com/article/
    fireproof-actor-kirk-cameron-shares-testimony-at-baptist-
    college/#.YlrFMtPMKmk.

3   "'The Biggest Celebrity Is Jesus'." Beliefnet. Last modified July
    27, 2017. https://www.beliefnet.com/entertainment/celebrities/
    the-biggest-celebrity-is-jesus.aspx.

4   "Ex Korn Drummer David Silveria: 'We Changed The Music
    Scene And Put The Course Of Heavy Music On A Different
    Route'." BLABBERMOUTH.NET. Last modified August 16,
    2020. https://www.blabbermouth.net/news/ex-korn-drummer-
    david-silveria-we-changed-the-music-scene-and-put-the-
    course-of-heavy-music-on-a-different-route/.

5   TBN. "Brian "Head" Welch (KORN): Overcoming Addiction
    and Finding Jesus | FULL EPISODE | Praise on TBN."
    YouTube. August 31, 2021. https://www.youtube.com/
    watch?v=MGwRtfLpFhE..

6 jesuschangeslives. "Brian Welch: From Korn to Jesus."
   YouTube. August 22, 2008. https://www.youtube.com/
   watch?v=Fs7i_ckEHVA.

7 jesuschangeslives. "Brian Welch: From Korn to Jesus."
   YouTube. August 22, 2008. https://www.youtube.com/
   watch?v=Fs7i_ckEHVA.

8 "Princess Sarah Culberson of Sierra Leone - Princess Sarah
   Culberson." Princess Sarah Culberson. Accessed February 11,
   2022. https://sarahculberson.com/.

9 Adams, Char. "In Quest to Find Birth Family, Woman Makes
   'life-Altering' Discovery: She's a Princess." NBC News. Last
   modified December 17, 2020. https://www.nbcnews.com/news/
   nbcblk/quest-find-birth-family-woman-makes-life-altering-
   discovery-she-n1251296.

10 Adams, Char. "In Quest to Find Birth Family, Woman Makes
    'life-Altering' Discovery: She's a Princess." NBC News. Last
    modified December 17, 2020. https://www.nbcnews.com/news/
    nbcblk/quest-find-birth-family-woman-makes-life-altering-
    discovery-she-n1251296.

11 Adams, Char. "In Quest to Find Birth Family, Woman Makes
    'life-Altering' Discovery: She's a Princess." NBC News. Last
    modified December 17, 2020. https://www.nbcnews.com/news/
    nbcblk/quest-find-birth-family-woman-makes-life-altering-
    discovery-she-n1251296.

12 Adams, Char. "In Quest to Find Birth Family, Woman Makes
    'life-Altering' Discovery: She's a Princess." NBC News. Last
    modified December 17, 2020. https://www.nbcnews.com/news/
    nbcblk/quest-find-birth-family-woman-makes-life-altering-
    discovery-she-n1251296.

13 "Princess Sarah Culberson of Sierra Leone - Princess Sarah

Culberson." Princess Sarah Culberson. Accessed February 11, 2022. https://sarahculberson.com/.

14   "Princess Sarah Culberson of Sierra Leone - Princess Sarah Culberson." Princess Sarah Culberson. Accessed February 11, 2022. https://sarahculberson.com/.

15   "What Celebrities Would Look Like If Their Distinctive Features Were Missing." Bright Side. Last modified May 10, 2017. https://brightside.me/wonder-people/what-celebrities-would-look-like-if-their-distinctive-features-were-missing-332810/.

16   Richman-Abdou, Kelly. "Kintsugi, a Centuries-Old Japanese Method of Repairing Pottery with Gold." My Modern Met. Last modified March 5, 2022. https://mymodernmet.com/kintsugi-kintsukuroi/.

17   Cole, Mark. "Mark Cole: Find Your Sweet Spot." John C. Maxwell. Last modified November 22, 2019. https://www.johnmaxwell.com/blog/mark-cole-find-your-sweet-spot/.

18   Arter, Melanie. "Ben Carson: 'Everybody Called Me Dummy' in School." CNS News. Accessed September 13, 2022. https://www.cnsnews.com/news/article/melanie-hunter/ben-carson-everybody-called-me-dummy-school.

19   Carson, Ben. Gifted Hands. Grand Rapids: Zondervan, 2008.

20   Encyclopædia Britannica Online. s.v. "Ben Carson," accessed February 22, 2022 , https://www.britannica.com/biography/Ben-Carson.

21   Carson, Ben. Gifted Hands. Grand Rapids: Zondervan, 2008.

22   TheFreeDictionary.com. s.v."impact zone," accessed February 1, 2022, https://www.thefreedictionary.com/impact+zone.

23   Carson, Ben, and Cecil Murphey. Think Big: Unleashing Your Potential for Excellence. Grand Rapids: Zondervan, 2009.

24 Carson, Ben. Gifted Hands. Grand Rapids: Zondervan, 2008.

25 Straeter, Kelsey. "Lauren Daigle Reveals She Suffered from 2 Years of "Extreme Illness" Before Music Healed Her." Faithit. Last modified April 18, 2019. https://faithit.com/lauren-daigle-reveals-suffered-2-years-extreme-illness-music-healed/.

26 Daigle, Lauren. "Lauren Daigle: God Showed Me My Future." Guideposts. Last modified January 23, 2019. https://www.guideposts.org/better-living/entertainment/music/lauren-daigle-god-showed-me-my-future.

27 Daigle, Lauren. "Lauren Daigle: God Showed Me My Future" Guideposts. Last modified January 23, 2019. https://www.guideposts.org/better-living/entertainment/music/lauren-daigle-god-showed-me-my-future.

28 Sweeten-Shults, Lana. "Illness, 'no' on 'American Idol' Didn't Stop Daigle." GCU News. Last modified September 25, 2019. https://news.gcu.edu/2019/09/lauren-daigle-concert-grand-canyon-university/.

29 Gunner, Jennifer. "How Did Martin Luther King's Vision Change the World?" Biography Articles & Resources | YourDictionary. Accessed February 11, 2022. https://biography.yourdictionary.com/articles/martin-luther-kings-vision-change-world.html.

30 "Tony Dungy." Pro Football Hall of Fame. Accessed February 15, 2022. https://www.profootballhof.com/players/tony-dungy/.

31 NFL. "Tony Dungy (Bucs/Colts, HC) Career Feature | 2016 Pro Football Hall of Fame | NFL." YouTube. August 5, 2016. https://www.youtube.com/watch?v=ARX-aRRlBlo.

32 Jesus Calling Devotional & Podcast. "Winning Isn't Everything—Jesus Is: Tony Dungy and Sam Acho." YouTube. January 14, 2021. https://www.youtube.com/watch?v=MDz3fqToekU.

33   FCA Resources. "Common Enemies (Teamwork - Chapter 1)." FCA Resources. Last modified January 1, 2009. https://fcaresources.com/devotional/common-enemies-teamwork-chapter-1.

34   Jon Gordon's Positive University. "Tips for Life, Teamwork and Success." Podcast audio. June 2018. https://positiveuniversity.com/episode/tony-dungy/.

35   Jesus Calling Devotional & Podcast. "Winning Isn't Everything—Jesus Is: Tony Dungy and Sam Acho." YouTube. January 14, 2021. https://www.youtube.com/watch?v=MDz3fqToekU.

36   FCA Resources. "Common Enemies (Teamwork - Chapter 1)." FCA Resources. Last modified January 1, 2009. https://fcaresources.com/devotional/common-enemies-teamwork-chapter-1.

37   Dungy, Tony, and Nathan Whitaker. Quiet Strength: A Memoir. Tyndale Momentum, 2007.

38   Jon Gordon's Positive University. "Tips for Life, Teamwork and Success." Podcast audio. June 2018. https://positiveuniversity.com/episode/tony-dungy/.

39   "Name Meaning Tessa." Kidadl. Accessed April 11, 2022. https://kidadl.com/baby-names/meaning-of/tessa.

40   Lewis, Brenda R. Kings & Queens: A Chronicle of History's Most Interesting Monarchies. Amber Books, 2017.

41   Meares, Hadley. "The Delusion That Made Nobles Think Their Bodies Were Made of Glass." HISTORY. Last modified August 29, 2018. https://www.history.com/news/the-delusion-that-made-nobles-think-their-bodies-were-made-of-glass.

42   "The Weeping of the Vines." Bodegas Piqueras. Last modified

February 1, 2016. https://www.bodegaspiqueras.com/en/
el-llanto-de-las-vinas/.

43 Hayes, Bethany. "Learn How to Prune Grape Vines for a
Fruitful Harvest." MorningChores. Accessed April 11, 2022.
https://morningchores.com/pruning-grape-vines/.

44 Foster, Michèle. "When Grapevines Cry." Soliere.
Last modified April 1, 2019. https://www.soliere.com/
post/2019/04/02/when-grapevines-cry.

45 Hayes, Bethany. "Learn How to Prune Grape Vines for a
Fruitful Harvest." MorningChores. Accessed April 11, 2022.
https://morningchores.com/pruning-grape-vines/.

46 Stancil, Joanna M. "The Power of One Tree - The
Very Air We Breathe" USDA. Last modified June 3,
2019. https://www.usda.gov/media/blog/2015/03/17/
power-one-tree-very-air-we-breathe.

47 American Society of Hematology. "Blood Basics." In
Hematology Glossary. Washington, DC: Hematology.org, n.d.
Accessed February 23, 2022. https://www.hematology.org/
education/patients/blood-basics.

48 Mlynek, Alex. "6 Magical Ways That Breastmilk Changes to
Meet Your Baby's Needs." Today's Parent. Accessed February
23, 2022. https://www.todaysparent.com/baby/breastfeeding/
magical-ways-breastmilk-changes-to-meet-your-babys-needs/.

49 Dumke, Kimberly. "The Power of the Sun." National
Geographic Society. Accessed April 13, 2022. https://
education.nationalgeographic.org/resource/power-sun.

50 Severance, Ph.D., Diane. "Evangelical Revival in England."
Christianity.com. Last modified May 3, 2010. https://www.
christianity.com/church/church-history/timeline/1701-1800/
evangelical-revival-in-england-11630228.html.

51   DeSelm, Dave. "Do It Again, Lord." Dave DeSelm Ministries. Last modified April 21, 2021. https://www.davedeselmministries.org/devotionals/do-it-again-lord.

52   Gomez, Tony. "Hatching Butterflies...a Monarch Emerges From A Chrysalis!" Monarch Butterfly Garden- Bring Home the Butterflies. Last modified September 7, 2019. https://monarchbutterflygarden.net/hatching-butterflies-Monarch-emerges-chrysalis/.

53   Jomard, Asa. "What Happens Inside the Chrysalis of a Butterfly?" Sciencing. Last modified November 22, 2019, https://sciencing.com/happens-inside-chrysalis-butterfly-8148799.html.

54   Abhinandhinee. "Bethany Hamilton | The Success Story of a Surfer Who Faced a Near-Death Experience." Failure Before Success. Last modified October 12, 2021. https://failurebeforesuccess.com/bethany-hamilton/.

55   Hamilton, Bethany. "Called to Be You." Bethany Hamilton (blog). October 20, 2020. https://bethanyhamilton.com/called-to-be-you/.

56   ABC News. "The Epic Journey of NFL's Michael Oher." YouTube. December 30, 2009. https://www.youtube.com/watch?v=iwE1iXf_3ao.

57   ABC News. "The Epic Journey of NFL's Michael Oher." YouTube. December 30, 2009. https://www.youtube.com/watch?v=iwE1iXf_3ao.

58   ABC News. "The Epic Journey of NFL's Michael Oher." YouTube. December 30, 2009. https://www.youtube.com/watch?v=iwE1iXf_3ao.

59   ABC News. "The Epic Journey of NFL's Michael Oher." YouTube. December 30, 2009. https://www.youtube.com/watch?v=iwE1iXf_3ao.

60   "The Tough Story of Michael Oher, Who Inspired the Film 'The Blind Side'." Bright Side. Accessed January 12, 2022. https://brightside.me/wonder-people/the-tough-story-of-michael-oher-who-inspired-the-film-the-blind-side-796565/.

61   Oher, Michael. I Beat the Odds: From Homelessness, to The Blind Side, and Beyond. London: Penguin, 2012.

62   Author Unknown, "The Elephant and the Rope."

63   "Edison Quotes." Thomas Edison. Accessed April 13, 2022. https://www.thomasedison.org/edison-quotes.

64   Dryjanski, Alexandra. "Helen Keller: An Inspiration." ASL American Sign Language. Last modified May 2, 2012. https://www.lifeprint.com/asl101/topics/helen-keller-inspiration.htm.

65   Know the ADA. "The Life and Lessons of Helen Keller." Know the ADA. Accessed February 23, 2022. https://know-the-ada.com/t4/life-lessons-hellen-keller.html.

66   Olson, Jeff. The Slight Edge. Austin: Greenleaf Book Group, 2013.

67   Oher, Michael. I Beat the Odds: From Homelessness, to The Blind Side, and Beyond. London: Penguin, 2012.

68   Christian Broadcasting Network. "Zach Hunter: The Teenage Abolitionist." CBN.com. Accessed January 17, 2022. https://www1.cbn.com/700club/zach-hunter-teenage-abolitionist.

69   Christian Broadcasting Network. "Zach Hunter: The Teenage Abolitionist." CBN.com. Accessed January 17, 2022. https://www1.cbn.com/700club/zach-hunter-teenage-abolitionist.

70   Zondervan. "Zach Hunter on Be The Change." YouTube. March 12, 2012. https://www.youtube.com/watch?v=BBIXS1tkO9w.

71   Christian Broadcasting Network. "Zach Hunter: The Teenage

Abolitionist." CBN.com. Accessed January 17, 2022. https://www1.cbn.com/700club/zach-hunter-teenage-abolitionist.

72   Smith, Peter. "Billy Graham Credited Fiery Kentucky Preacher for Inspiring Him to Become Evangelist." Courier Journal. February 21, 2018. https://www.courier-journal.com/story/news/local/2018/02/21/billy-graham-credited-kentucky-preacher-becoming-evangelist/359969002/.

73   wikiHow Staff. "3 Ways to Become Famous." WikiHow. Accessed April 2, 2020. https://www.wikihow.com/Become-Famous.

74   wikiHow Staff. "3 Ways to Become Famous." WikiHow. Accessed April 2, 2020. https://www.wikihow.com/Become-Famous.

75   wikiHow Staff. "3 Ways to Become Famous." WikiHow. Accessed April 2, 2020. https://www.wikihow.com/Become-Famous.

76   wikiHow Staff. "3 Ways to Become Famous." WikiHow. Accessed April 2, 2020. https://www.wikihow.com/Become-Famous.

77   Rainey, Dennis and Barbara. "Five Essentials to Leaving a Legacy That Will Outlive You." FamilyLife®. Accessed January 19, 2022. https://www.familylife.com/articles/topics/parenting/foundations/godly-legacy/five-essentials-to-leaving-a-legacy-that-will-outlive-you/.